CW00434345

Insp
Women

Created as a woman

Beverley Shepherd

Copyright © CWR 2007

Published 2007 by CWR, Waverley Abbey House, Waverley Lane, Farnham, Surrey
GU9 8EP, UK. Registered Charity No. 294387. Registered Limited Company No.
1990308.

The right of Beverley Shepherd to be identified as the author of this work has been
asserted by her in accordance with the Copyright, Designs and Patents Act 1988,
sections 77 and 78.

See back of book for list of National Distributors.

Unless otherwise indicated, all Scripture references are from the Holy Bible: New
International Version (NIV), copyright © 1973, 1978, 1984 by the International Bible
Society.

Concept development, editing, design and production by CWR

Cover image: Getty/BLOOMimage

Printed in Finland by WS Bookwell

ISBN: 978-1-85345-450-9

Contents

Introduction

Woman's story begins in the creative mind of God. He chose, by a deliberate creative act, to make woman. 'Then the LORD God made a woman from the rib he had taken out of the man …' (Gen. 2:22). His creation was not complete until a woman walked in the Garden of Eden. We were and are part of God's wonderful creation plan – no accident, no mistake. The Genesis account is quite clear – woman is similar to but different from the man. This throws up many questions for those of us seeking to be the woman God created us to be: What does it mean to be a woman? How is this different from being a man? Is there a blueprint for living as a woman of God? … and so the questions go on.

Over the years I have noticed within myself a desire for clear answers and yet, as I've talked with others, meditated on God's Word and read different books I have discovered that becoming the woman God created me to be is a journey and not a destination. It is a 'becoming' and no one fixed thing at any time. My journey and yours will be different, and so the reflections offered in this book may, in some way, correspond to points on your own journey, or may provide thoughts for consideration where our journeys differ.

I have sought to follow the biblical themes of creation, the Fall, redemption, being chosen, transformation and glory, trusting that this theological flow will give insight into our own journeys. Yet my prayer is that we move beyond mere insight – understanding what God is saying to us about being a woman will only be helpful in as far as it is grounded in a relationship with Him. The most vital part of my own journey is the deep knowledge that I am loved – totally, unconditionally, unchangeably and eternally – by my heavenly husband. It is within the warmth and security of this love that we have the confidence to look at who we are, the courage to bring our wounded, damaged places into the light for His healing, and the desire to relinquish our self-protective strategies that surround us with a hard shell, so that we can feel the tenderness of His touch. These things do not happen overnight – they occur as relationship grows, trust deepens and as we increasingly long for a heart that reflects His own.

Sometimes the circumstances of our lives or the dictates of our culture make being a woman hard, painful or even dangerous. That was never God's plan. Matthew Henry's commentary is, I believe, closer to God's intention:

> ... *the woman was made of a rib out of the side of Adam; not made out of his head to rule over him, nor out of his feet to be trampled upon by him, but out of his side to be equal with him, under his arm to be protected, and near his heart to be beloved.*[1]

The reality of many women's experience is not that of being equal, protected or loved, and so the journey towards rediscovering and then revealing our own woman's heart will involve many setbacks – the temptations to hide our heart, to rebuild self-protective walls and to deny our own femininity will face us on a daily basis. God's words to Joshua 'Be strong and courageous' (Josh. 1:9) could equally apply to us as we seek, with God's guidance and love, to reclaim the promised land of our own heart.

A prayer

> So God created man in his own image,
> in the image of God he created him;
> male and female he created them.

(Genesis 1:27)

Lord,
Thank you that when you formed me in my mother's womb
You made me a woman.
I'm a woman who works in a man's world – and most days
that's fine.
Most days it's fun.

But every now and then … I notice …
I notice the professional shell I have put around myself
I notice the sharp words I use to shield my vulnerability
I notice the desensitising that protects me from hurt
I notice the temptation to hide my femininity –
Especially when others ignore or devalue me as a woman.

Thank you that you see me
Thank you that I am precious and honoured in your sight
Thank you that your oil and wine tenderise my toughened
skin
And you, O Lord Most High, are all the protection I need.
Thank you that you see and celebrate your creation – your
woman – me!

Today, help me to remember and enjoy
The woman you created me to be.
Amen[2]

For reflection

I invite you to spend time considering these questions:

- How do you feel about being a woman?

- What makes you thankful for your gender?

- What aspects of being a woman do you find hard?

- What does your woman's heart long for?

Chapter 1

Created as a woman

*'So God created man in his own image, in the
image of God he created him; male and
female he created them.'*
Genesis 1:27

Created by God and for God

Like all good stories the story of woman begins with those familiar words: 'In the beginning …'. Genesis 1:1 goes on to say '… God created'. Our existence flows out of the mind, heart and creative activity of God. God wanted daughters and when He created you and me He wasn't 'hoping for a boy'! He made us different from men and that difference is to be valued because God values it. In fact, it is not only to be valued, it is needed – God's world needs what we can offer as women. If I fail to understand what I have to offer, if I have been taught to devalue or even hate my femininity, then the world is the poorer.

Created from the rib of Adam, who was himself created from the dust of the ground, Eve's life flows from the life God breathed into Adam – it is God's breath or spirit that defines woman as a living being. God made us as women and He made us for Himself. As St Augustine put it over fifteen hundred years ago in his *Confessions*: 'Thou hast made us for Thyself, and our heart is restless till it finds its rest in Thee.'

Good friends of mine have recently had their first child – a beautiful girl named Lily. Watching the face of her father, Ian, as he looks at his daughter is a joy – delight, protectiveness and love register in every glance of his eyes towards her. Yet this is surely a pale reflection of how our Father God looks at us. We are told that after each stage in the creation story God stopped and looked at what He had made. God 'saw'. When man and woman are created God 'sees' them – and in that seeing a gift of recognition, of honour and worth is bestowed. As God sees, He celebrates: 'It is good – it is very good'. The word 'good' means more than 'well made' – it carries with it a sense of beauty, of being pleasing. At the very moment of her creation woman is seen and celebrated – she knows what it is to be truly beautiful – to be looked at with love and complete satisfaction. She knows what it is to stand before God without shame, enjoying His pleasure and delight.

Although no woman since Eve (I will refer to the woman as Eve, even though she was not given this name until after the Fall) has experienced what it means to be seen and celebrated in such totality, we each of us desire to be truly beautiful – to be celebrated. John and Stasi Eldredge in *Captivating* write:

> *A woman in her glory, a woman of beauty, is a woman who is not striving to become beautiful or worthy or enough. She knows in her quiet center where God dwells that he finds her beautiful, has deemed her worthy, and in him, she is enough.*[1]

Some of the most beautiful women I know have grey hairs and wrinkled faces – their beauty shines from within. Laughter dances in their eyes and warmth perfumes their presence. Their beauty flows from the sure and certain knowledge that they are loved – both by their heavenly Father and by friends and family.

In His image …

When God created both man and woman, He created them in His image. As God is not a physical being – He has no physical body – this cannot mean a physical likeness. So what does it mean to be created in His image? It means that we resemble God in the way we have been put together. Selwyn Hughes says:

> *The Almighty paid the highest compliment he could ever pay to human beings when he made us like himself. God is a rational*

being who thinks. So are we. God is a volitional being who chooses.
So are we. God is an emotional being who feels. So are we.[2]

God is a spiritual being, full of creative energy – so are we. We also reflect His moral likeness – our character and behaviour were designed to be an exact representation of the character and behaviour of God. If you could have placed a camera in the Garden of Eden to observe Adam and Eve, you would have seen two people who reflected God's character and attitude in the way they treated each other (their relationships) and in the way they stewarded creation (their rule).

Created for relationship

Adam could not reflect the image of God alone for God is three Persons in a loving relationship with each other. 'In the beginning … the Word was with God, and … was God' (John 1:1). As D. Broughton Knox puts it:

> *The Father loves the Son and gives Him everything. The Son always does that which pleases the Father. The Spirit takes of the things of the Son and shows them to us. He does not glorify Himself. We learn from the Trinity that relationship is the essence of reality and therefore the essence of our existence, and we also learn that the way this relationship should be expressed is by concern for others. Within the Trinity itself there is a concern by the persons of the Trinity for one another.*[3]

At the centre of the Godhead is relationship and it is only as Adam responds to the woman God brings to him that he can begin to reflect God's relational image. He is to relate as the Trinity relates – with 'other-centredness' (a desire to serve and bless) and not from sinful self-interest. Eve was made following God's observation that it was not good for man to be alone and it is only with the creation of woman that God looks at what He has made and declares it 'very good'.

How then are we to relate as God relates? Let's look at how, before the Fall, Adam relates to the woman. 'This is now bone of my bones and flesh of my flesh; she shall be called "woman"...' (Gen. 2:23). Firstly he recognises their 'sameness' – she is 'bone of my bones and flesh of my flesh'. As we relate to others we must acknowledge our shared humanity and our equality in the sight of God – there are no grounds for thinking of ourselves as better than anyone else. Secondly, Adam respects their difference: 'she shall be called "woman" for she was taken out of man.' In 'woman' God has created a different and complementary being.

Only as our uniqueness and difference are respected by others do we dare to remove our protective mask and be 'naked' before them. 'The man and his wife were both naked, and they felt no shame' (Gen. 2:25). Why is their nakedness important? To say that we are created for relationship gives no hint of the richness of relationship which God intended – He designed us for intimacy, for the joy of knowing and being fully known.

Many of us have learned to fear intimacy: it is in our most intimate relationships where we are most vulnerable to hurt and rejection, so we hide. We hide behind our roles, our busyness, our 'ministry', our clothes and our other various defences. Adam and Eve knew what it was to be together, to be naked, without defence, and feel no shame. 'No shame' implies vulnerability without fear of criticism, rejection or being taken advantage of – totally open to another person. Larry Crabb says:

Imagine the pleasure that rushed through Eve's entire being when Adam first approached her. After looking at animals for so long, Adam must have been ecstatic when he saw woman, naked, beautiful, inviting. Certainly sexual arousal must have been wonderfully present, but Adam's enjoyment of Eve extended to every level of relationship … A woman wants to know that the deepest parts of her being are richly enjoyed by a man who will therefore treat her with tenderness and look at her with delight.[4]

God intends that these two similar and yet diverse beings should become a unified whole – just as the different Persons of the Trinity form one unified Godhead. The image of God can only truly be expressed through unity and community – we cannot reveal God's image in isolation.

At a 'Women in Mission' conference I met a woman who made a deep impression on me. Realising, from her unusual name, that I knew both her husband and son, I said 'Oh, you must be Michael's wife and Nat's mother.' I then apologised, remembering that some women dislike being referred to in this way. She smiled warmly at me and said: 'Beverley, I am very happy to be defined by my relationships!'

Created to rule

Together, Adam and Eve were to reflect the image of God in their rule over creation – they were given authority over every living creature (Gen. 1:28). To the casual observer this looks like 'absolute power' yet the reality is 'absolute surrender'. All true authority is delegated authority, as the account of the centurion in Luke 7 illustrates. Notice the centurion's right understanding of authority: 'I tell this one "Go" and he goes; and that one "Come" and he comes …' How is he able to do this? 'For I myself am a man under authority ...' (Luke 7:8). It is only as we are 'under authority' that we have authority – it is only those who are totally submitted to God who can rule in His image; whose rule is a reflection of God's character and His rule. It is an authority that seeks to bless and to protect: '... but you must not eat from the tree of the knowledge of good and evil, for when you eat of it you will surely die' (Gen. 2:17).

So this was Eve's role – co-ruler with Adam under God's rule – a position of privilege and authority. 'Authority' implies *'rightful, actual and unimpeded power to act, or to possess, control, use or dispose of, something or somebody'*.[5] Eve was given authority. All authority has limits or boundaries ('you must not eat from the tree') and to rule well we must respect these boundaries and submit to the one who has authority over us.

Larry Crabb points out that all authority is 'authority to serve' and not 'authority to lead' and suggests that women and men express their authority to serve differently.

A woman has been equipped to welcome others into relationship with her and to offer that welcome with a spirit secure enough to be non-demanding and confident enough to be thoroughly inviting.[6]

Esther exemplifies this. In a situation where her husband, the king, is being manipulated by the evil Haman and has issued a non-revocable edict that the Jews should be destroyed, she firstly invites others to pray and fast with her before she approaches the king: 'Go, gather together all the Jews who are in Susa, and fast for me. Do not eat or drink for three days, night or day. I and my maids will fast as you do' (Esth. 4:16). She invites others into a 'community of purpose' with her through prayer and fasting. She is also inviting God to guide

His people by creating the space in which His wisdom can be heard. When she does approach the king she is dependent on receiving his authority to even remain in His presence – her royal robes, outward signs of her authority as queen, are meaningless unless the king extends his gold sceptre towards her. The king not only raises his sceptre but offers her anything she wants – up to half his kingdom. Yet Esther is wise enough not to step outside the bounds of her own authority – the authority to invite and the authority to create atmosphere – and so she invites her husband to dinner and into relationship. She creates the atmosphere in which he is able to make wise decisions.

Similarly, in 1 Samuel 25 we see how Abigail exercises her authority through atmosphere and invitation. She gives clear direction to her servants, ensuring that food is sent on ahead for David and his men. On meeting with David she bows low before him with her face to the ground: she is not there to usurp his authority but to encourage him to use it wisely. She speaks with great humility and respect for his position, encouraging him to rethink his decision to slay every male in her household. His response: 'Praise be to the LORD, the God of Israel, who has sent you today to meet me. May you be blessed for your good judgment and for keeping me from bloodshed this day and from avenging myself with my own hands' (1 Sam. 25:32–33).

By contrast, Jezebel, wife of King Ahab, uses her authority to belittle her husband: 'Is this how you act as king over Israel?' (1 Kings 21:7) and to usurp his authority, writing letters in his name, and saying, 'I'll get you the vineyard of Naboth the Jezreelite'. The result – Ahab is held responsible for Naboth's death in God's eyes and judgment is passed on him via Elijah the prophet: 'In the place where dogs licked up Naboth's blood, dogs will lick up your blood – yes, yours!' (1 Kings 21:19). In the Bible, the name Jezebel becomes synonymous with women who usurp rightful authority, including God's authority. Not only does God rebuke those that allow her to do so, but she also is punished (Rev. 2:20–23).

Whilst we have to be careful not to usurp rightful authority, it seems to me that many women abdicate their authority. They neglect this aspect of God's image in them and 'hide' behind not only their fig leaf clothes but behind men. Pause and ask God to show you where He wants you to exercise authority. Is it in your work role, your home, your community, or your church? But remember: it is delegated authority, the true authority of one who is surrendered to the authority of God. It is the authority to serve.

The help-meet

When we read of God creating Eve, He calls her an *ezer kenegdo*. These words, often translated 'help-meet', are difficult to understand. Hebrew scholar Robert Alter translates them 'sustainer beside him'. The word *ezer* is interesting in its Old Testament usage: in addition to its use in the creation of Eve it's used only twenty other times. In each, it's God Himself who is being described, mostly in life or death contexts where God is the only hope.

My help comes from the LORD, the Maker of heaven and earth.

(Psa. 121:2)

May the LORD answer you when you are in distress, may the name of the God of Jacob protect you. May he send you help from the sanctuary and grant you support from Zion.

(Psa. 20:1–2)

We wait in hope for the LORD; he is our help and our shield.

(Psa. 33:20)

O house of Israel, trust in the LORD – he is their help and shield.
O house of Aaron, trust in the LORD – he is their help and shield.
You who fear him, trust in the LORD – he is their help and shield.

(Psa. 115:9–11)[7]

Knowing that we are created in God's image, it should not surprise us that built into our design is a role that God Himself embraces – the role of a life-saver or sustainer beside/alongside a man. Picture not a wimp but a warrior princess! A woman who will seek to sustain and protect those things that God values.

When I was young, I'd ask to accompany my brothers when they went out to play. My elder brother would complain to my mother: 'Mum, does she have to come along?' Having been told 'Yes' he would begrudgingly assign me some task to make my resented presence useful. Many women see their role in this way – an appendage, tolerated for her usefulness or 'help'. Yet our God created us for His delight, not because we were useful to Him. He gives us a role as an expression of our relationship with Him – not as a means of earning it.

Nor are we to be women who sap the strength of men through our neediness and constant demands. This is not who God created you and me to be! We're designed to fight alongside men in the spiritual battle for our families, communities, churches and workplaces. We are to take our rightful place as the 'sustainers alongside' men, knowing that we are an *essential* part of God's plan, with a role that He has fashioned into the very DNA of our being.

For reflection

•••

- Woman is an essential and wanted part of God's creation – God wanted daughters. How do you respond to that thought?

- At the heart of the Godhead is relationship. Take time to reflect on the importance of relationships in your own life.

- In what areas have you been given authority to rule, and how do you express that authority?

- In thinking about Esther and Abigail, are there areas where God would encourage you to exercise your authority over atmosphere and through invitation?

- Whether married or single, what does it mean to you to be a 'help-meet'?

Chapter 2

Woman and the Fall

'When the woman saw that the fruit of the tree was good for food
and pleasing to the eye, and also desirable for gaining wisdom,
she took some and ate it. She also gave some to her husband,
who was with her, and he ate it.'
Genesis 3:6

ve seems to have everything. She lives in a beautiful place, she has meaningful work stewarding God's creation, she has a husband with whom she is one, and together they walk with God in the cool of the evening. Yet this secure, loved woman is tempted. How can this be? What possible lure could the forbidden fruit hold for a woman whose life appears so complete?

At the root of her temptation is a doubt about the character of God. Is He holding out on her? Is He denying her the one thing that would make her life perfect? A doubt, planted by the serpent, that God Himself is not good. 'You won't die!' the serpent hisses, 'You will become like God, knowing good and evil.' Eve is convinced – the fruit looks so fresh and delicious … and it will make her wise. One helpful definition of sin is 'our attempt to supplement God's goodness'. And this is what we see Eve doing – taking what she believes a truly good God would have given her in the first place.

What do we do when we think that God is withholding the one thing that would make our lives complete? Eve takes matters into her own hands – she reaches out and takes the denied fruit. It is easy to point the finger at Eve, but the reality is that I know the same temptations: I too have doubted God's goodness, and so have you. Are we any different from Eve? When we perceive that there is something missing in our lives we are tempted to doubt God's goodness. Instead of trusting in the character of God, His timing and His love for us, we take the initiative and grasp at what we think we need to make life work.

Notice the heart of this temptation: 'to be like God'. Eve, you *are* like God – He made you in His image! You have His character written into your being and His life breath within you! Selwyn Hughes explains the pride that underlies this:

I have seen many recoil in unbelief when I told them that pride is
the desire to be God, because few have an awareness of a desire to
dethrone God ... Pride (if we let it) can soon persuade us our place
is to be the ruler rather than the subject. This is God's world and
we are his creatures. He built us that we might have a relationship
with himself, but our pride has led us to believe that we don't need
God and that it would be the greatest indignity to have to bow the
knee to him.[1]

What Eve really desires is autonomy: the freedom to take
what she wants when she wants it – freedom from dependence
on God. In choosing to eat the fruit, Eve is rejecting God's rule
in her life and declaring her autonomy – the freedom to make
her own decisions. The serpent's real deception is subtle: he
seems to offer freedom and life, but in reality Eve becomes
enslaved to her own sinful nature and has chosen spiritual
death.

God has already warned Adam that eating of the tree of
the knowledge of good and evil will lead to death. When God
said 'you will die' (Gen. 3:3), He was not speaking of physical
death alone. As a consequence of disobedience, the life of
God would be withdrawn from Adam and Eve – they would
become spiritually dead: 'darkened in their understanding and
separated from the life of God' (Eph. 4:18) and 'dead in [their]
transgressions and sins' (Eph. 2:1).

This is true for each one of us – we are born in the image
of Adam and the life of God has been withdrawn. Like light
bulbs disconnected from the electricity supply, we have lost the
capability to shine with God's life. Created in God's image and
likeness, the potential and desire to do good remains but the
power to live such a life has gone. We are disconnected from
the power source by our sin, our character no longer reflecting

the image of God.

In the next chapter we will be exploring what it means to be reconnected – through the rejection of Eve's strategy of self-determination and independence, and the renouncing of our perceived 'right' to live life on our own terms. We will consider how, in repentance and humility, we can submit ourselves to God's rule and ask to be connected to His power supply – the Holy Spirit. No woman can serve two masters – we cannot serve both God and our own sinful nature.

The effects of this rebellion against God and His rule are far-reaching. His image in us is now corrupted and that corruption extends to our relationships and our rule.

Relationships destroyed

In God's original purposes, Eve is created to be Adam's *ezer kenegdo*: 'one who comes alongside to sustain life'. This wonder-fully created woman is designed to be the answer to Adam's loneliness and to bring him life. Yet we read in Genesis 3 that it is Eve who falls prey to the serpent's tempting to eat of the forbidden fruit and then offers it to Adam – and so she brings him death: 'She also gave some to her husband, who was with her, and he ate it' (Gen. 3:6). As John and Stasi Eldredge comment in their book, *Captivating*, the Hebrew for 'who was with her' means 'right there at her side'. Adam isn't off doing the gardening when Eve is tempted by Satan, in the guise of a serpent – he is there with her, listening to every word the serpent is saying. Does he challenge the serpent's lies? Does he protect Eve from temptation and encourage her to trust in God's goodness? Does he remind her of God's clear instructions to them both? No! He is passive, silent, inert – he fails to be a husband who fights for her very life at the point she needs him most. The result: 'in Adam all die' (1 Cor. 15:22). Adam is held accountable before God for sin entering the world. Adam doesn't quite see it like this. He blames Eve and God ('the woman *you* put here with me' – Gen. 3:12, my italics). Eve blames the serpent.

Adam and Eve hide from God and, in many senses, from each other. Their relationship becomes a tangled mess of blame and shame. For Eve, the very relationship that was designed to counter any sense of 'aloneness' – her relationship with her husband – now becomes cursed with relational heartache, with the urge to control, and with the dominance of Adam ('he will rule over you' – Gen. 3:16). Her deep desire for intimacy will never be met in a lasting way – she is now alone, even within her marriage.

Similarly, for each of us a vicious relational cycle develops. We do not trust in God's goodness and so look to others to meet our needs. They fail us. Then, in coming to the realisation that no relationship can ever fully meet our need for intimacy we face two equal and opposite dangers. Firstly, we can blame the other person for not meeting our needs and demand that they change. Through demandingness and manipulation we seek to force others to meet our needs. Secondly, we can attempt to kill our heart's longing for intimacy in order to remain 'safe' and 'in control' – refusing any sense of vulnerability. This can be accompanied by 'perfectionism': the belief that my needs will be met when I am perfect enough to attract the right person to give me all that I need. Both paths lead to frustration and rejection, both of ourselves and of others.

Twelve years ago, I was given the wonderful privilege of preaching at my youngest brother's wedding. I prayed long and hard about what God would have me say to my brother and his wife-to-be. At one point I described to them the favourite toy of one of our nephews – a box with many shaped holes, some square, some round, others triangles or stars. Each differently-shaped brick would only fit through the hole shaped specifically for it. My point was that too often we expect others, especially our marriage partners, to fit through a certain-shaped hole and meet a need that they were never designed to meet. God has placed a God-shaped hole in our hearts and only He can fill it.

Running on empty

When the path of self-determination runs its course we reach its final conclusion – emptiness. 'My people have committed two sins: They have forsaken me, the spring of living water, and have dug their own cisterns, broken cisterns that cannot hold water' (Jer. 2:13). Selwyn Hughes writes:

> *So we were made with a thirst within which no water of earth can satisfy; an ache within which only God can assuage; a hunger unmet except by the food that comes from above… We may pour things into the containers of our lives, but for some reason they never seem to get filled. We are always partly empty; and for that reason we experience a profound awareness of a lack of fullness and happiness.*[2]

A few years ago I had the opportunity to run a series of leadership training courses for United Airlines pursers. This involved spending the week in the United States and co-training with others who were involved in the project. One week, my co-trainer was a delightful lady named Sue. As Sue and I got to know each other she asked more and more questions about my faith in God and the impact it had on my life. At one point

I remember challenging her as to why she wanted to know: 'Sue, you seem to have everything that many women would seek: a happy marriage, a lovely child, a fulfilling job, a nice house, good friends and enough money in the bank to be very comfortable. Why are you so interested in God?' Her reply was instructive: 'Because deep down I know that there is something missing.' In her own way, Sue was saying, 'I know I look full, but deep down I'm empty.'

Recorded in John's Gospel is the story of the Samaritan woman at the well (John 4:1–42). She knew what it was to be empty – she had had five husbands and the man she was now living with was not her husband. Her strategy for making life work – a series of relationships with different men – had failed to satisfy. So when Jesus talks to her of drinking living water and never thirsting again, she says: 'Sir, give me this water so that I won't get thirsty ...' (v.15).

It sounds too good to be true – no more hard work of coming to collect water each day, and never thirsting again. Of course she wants it! But first Jesus confronts her with her cracked cistern: 'Go, call your husband and come back' (v.16). Now she starts to hedge and diverts the conversation to a theological debate about worship. She has realised that in order to access the living water she will have to renounce her own life strategies – and the realisation is uncomfortable. It's a choice she makes though, and 'leaving her water jar' (v.28) she experiences what it means for the water Jesus gives to become 'a spring of water welling up to eternal life' (v.14) when many in the town believe because of her testimony.

Often it isn't until the cracked cisterns of our own life strategies have run dry that we seek the living water offered by God. Jesus is willing to give each one of us living water but there is a cost – total surrender. When my co-trainer, Sue, realised this she very honestly said: 'I've realised that the relationship with God that you have been speaking about, Bev, is as serious as marriage. I'm not ready to give up my "singleness" yet.'

To drink from the spring of living water we have to stop digging our own cisterns – our personal strategies to make life work – and turn in dependency to God as our source of supply.

Life-bearers – and pain

Although our closest relationships are now a tangled web of self-protection, vulnerability, pride, shame, love and hate, God still blesses them with fruitfulness. 'Adam lay with his wife Eve, and she became pregnant and gave birth to Cain' (Gen. 4:1). In fact it is through their offspring that redemption will come: '… he will crush your [the serpent's] head …' (Gen. 3:15).

The story is told of a schoolboy who was asked to write an essay on birth for his homework. He decided to ask his mother how he was born. With embarrassment and somewhat hesitantly she replied, 'When we decided that we wanted a baby we asked God for one, and a stork brought you to us and left you on our doorstep.' He then went to his grandmother and asked how his mummy had been born. His grandmother looked rather embarrassed too and, after a bit of umming and erring, said, 'Well, when your Grandpa and I wanted to have a baby, we asked God for one. The next morning, when we looked out into the garden, there was your mother – a little baby lying underneath the gooseberry bush.' 'And what about you, Grandma?' the child persisted. 'Were you born in the same way?' 'That's right, dear, I was' she replied. The lad then went off and started to write: 'In the last three generations there have not been any natural births in our family …'[3]

As Eve's daughters, the vocation of all women is to be a mother – to bring life into this world. This call is not confined to physical reproduction and so is in no way limited by singleness or infertility. One of the most famous 'mothers' of our generation never bore a single child: Mother Theresa. Yet she and her sisters brought life into the heart of Calcutta – a city named after the goddess, Kali, who is often associated with death and destruction.

We are called to be life-bearers – into our homes, our communities, our churches, our schools and our workplaces. Yet, in Genesis 3:16 we read: 'I will greatly increase your pains in childbearing; with pain you will give birth to children.' What does this pain refer to if it's not the physical pain of muscles contracting to push a child into the world? For a woman to bring life into a situation she has to face her own vulnerability, risking rejection and emotional pain.

When God called me into a role that involved standing and speaking in front of groups of people (sometimes numbering hundreds), He showed me the choice I had to make. Would I be real? Most speakers can stand in front of a group and entertain or educate, but my calling as a woman is to bring forth life. I can only do this if I am prepared to come out of hiding, abandon the mask, and be real and vulnerable – risking misunderstanding and rejection. Every time I step onto the platform I face this choice. And so do you! Each day God asks, 'Will you be a life-bearer or will you hide?' 'Will you walk into your town, your workplace, your various social meetings, your family – and bring life?'

We bring life in a variety of ways, through a smile, a caring act, a kind word; through wise insight that brings light into the darkest situation, through courageous challenge and sacrificial giving – allowing the life of Jesus to be clothed in our ordinary lives. One Christian business woman tells of a particular meeting of the sales team of which she was a part. The only other woman in this predominantly male team boasted of a sales presentation she had managed to secure for the following day with a very prestigious potential new customer. This woman was generally disliked within the team and her sales techniques viewed suspiciously, as she was thought to use her gender inappropriately. So instead of her announcement being greeted with enthusiasm, there was a general lack of response. The next morning, whilst reading her Bible on the way to work, the Christian woman was challenged to rethink her attitude towards her colleague. She purchased some flowers and, with some embarrassment, left them on the desk of her fellow saleswoman with a note wishing her well in her sales presentation. Twenty minutes later her colleague appeared at her office door, tears glistening on her cheeks. 'Thank you so much for the flowers – I didn't think anyone cared.' Vulnerability and obedience had brought forth life.

Many women allow their life-bearing role as a mother to be limited to within their own families, whilst others have thought that their lack of ability or opportunity to bear natural children means that this role is denied to them. God calls all of us, as women, to be mothers – nurturing life in every setting in which He places us.

In God's wonderful grace, fallen Eve still has a place in His purposes – she is to be the 'mother of all the living' (Gen. 3:20). In fulfilling her role she will know pain, but it's a pain that will be forgotten in the joy of new life!

'It's not too late ...'

In Eve, before the Fall, we have seen the woman we were created to be – a woman who reflected God's image in her attitudes, emotions, actions and relationships. Yet, when we look in the mirror this is not the woman who stares back. Our life history is written on our faces – however skilful we are with the make-up!

Jesus died for us *before* we became who we are! Our story begins before time was created, with a crucifixion: Jesus, 'slain from the creation of the world' (Rev. 13:8).

We do not have to hide the truth of who we are from Him. He died for Eve before she was tempted and ate the fruit. He looks at the fallen women we are and says: 'It is not too late – through My death God's image in you can be restored. Your true identity as God's beloved daughter can be revealed. Will you hand over control of your life to Me and allow Me to transform you?'

> *And yet I know that long ago you made a fairy-tale for me,*
> *About the day when you would take your sword*
> *And battle through the thicket of the things I have become.*
> *You'll kiss to life my sleeping beauty waiting*
> *For her prince to come.*[4]

For reflection

- Do you believe that God is withholding something from you – something that in your eyes would make your life complete?

- What makes it difficult to trust God in this area?

- Take time over the next week to identify strategies you are tempted to adopt to have your needs met.

- Reflect on the demandingness, control and perfectionism you experience in your relationships with others.

- Speak out your thanks to God for the good relationships He has gifted you with.

- Reflect on your call to be a life-bearer and what this means in the different contexts of your life.

Chapter 3

Woman redeemed

*'But now, this is what the Lord says – he who
created you, O Jacob, he who formed you, O Israel;
"Fear not, for I have redeemed you; I have summoned
you by name; you are mine."'*
Isaiah 43:1

'm a born romantic. The basic plot of all good romances seems very similar – in the beginning all is well, the heroine is living a happy life. Enter stage left, the villain – be it wicked stepmother, cruel landlord, evil witch or seducing stranger. The heroine is captured and imprisoned. Dressed in rags, she now works to the point of exhaustion, disillusioned and hopeless, unable to save herself. She needs someone to fight for her; someone who can see past the dirty rags and love her for who she really is.

When Eve was seduced by the serpent, Adam was passive: he failed to fight for her. Jesus, the second Adam, battles for us. Sin believes that it has locked us up and thrown away the key, end of story. Not so! The good news is that Father God has sent Jesus 'to bind up the broken-hearted, to proclaim freedom for the captives and release from darkness for the prisoners …' (Isa. 61:1).

Many of us have welcomed Jesus as He unlocks and opens the prison door. Yet, instead of allowing Him to lead us out into a life of purpose and challenge, we are content to stay securely in our open cell. It's as if Cinderella, having been sought out by the prince, is content to return to her cellar, still dressed in rags, warmed by the thought that the prince loves her. Yet the prince wants to take her to his palace. He wants her beside him as he rules his kingdom; he wants to see her dressed in her royal robes, exercising the authority she now has through her relationship with him. He invites her to share his life.

What Adam and Eve forfeited through disobedience – the life of God in them – Jesus offers to restore. He invites us to exchange death for life, cracked cisterns for living water, darkness for light, and futility for purpose. This exchange is both an event and a journey. A former Archbishop of Canterbury was accosted by a rather zealous student whilst walking in the city of Durham. 'Are you saved?' the student loudly demanded. With great graciousness, the archbishop quietly replied: 'By God's grace I have been saved, I am being saved and I will be saved.' Like the people of Israel, many of us can point to a time when we left Egypt, when we were 'converted', yet the journey of 'becoming' had only just started. Transformation into the people of God took the Israelites through the desert and into the promised land – it involved setbacks, warfare, rebellion and blessing.

How will we know when we have been fully transformed? When we look like Christ who was and is 'the radiance of God's glory and the exact representation of his being' (Heb. 1:3). This is our hope and God's promise: '…we, who with unveiled faces all reflect the Lord's glory, are being transformed into his likeness …' (2 Cor. 3:18). It is not an event but a process – a process that God will bring to completion in eternity.

The enemy would want to hiss: 'This is not for you. You are beyond hope – God's image has been obliterated in your life.' He is a liar. God, who in Genesis 1 created something out of nothing, is able to take your life and mine and transform them so that we too can reflect His glory.

The time has come!

When His public ministry begins, Jesus spells out His agenda: 'The time has come … The kingdom of God is near. Repent and believe the good news!' (Mark 1:15).

The 'kingdom of God' is shorthand for the rule of God. Jesus declares that God's rule over this earth is about to be re-established. Good news indeed. But this is not an army of occupation, it is an intimate invitation: 'Will you appoint God as your King?'

How do we do that? We repent of self-rule. Many people repent of 'sins' – acts of disobedience committed – without ever repenting of the heart attitude that lies at the root of them. This is an attitude which declares 'I have the right to determine my own life'. Repentance is not a suggestion but a command. 'In the past God overlooked such ignorance, but now he commands all people everywhere to repent' (Acts 17:30).

The word translated 'repent' in English is the Greek word '*metanoeo*'. '*Meta*' means 'to change' and '*nous*' means 'the mind'. Asking God to forgive your sins without 'changing your mind' is not repentance but remorse. A change of mind must lead to a change of behaviour: if there has been no change of behaviour, then it would be wise to question whether there has been any change of mind. Yet, when we truly repent, God forgives and purifies us (1 John 1:9). He enables us, through the strengthening of His Spirit, to change our actions.

Is there a woman alive who believes that she is fully the person God designed her to be? We look into the mirror and see fault – and not just with our physical selves. We see hardness where God intends vulnerability; selfishness where He intends generosity; a critical spirit where He intends warm invitation; control and efficiency instead of fruitfulness; demandingness of others where He intends dependence on Him. 'For all have sinned and fall short of the glory of God' (Rom. 3:23).

You and I have no power to change ourselves – not the transformational change God is looking for. All we can do is to die. 'I tell you the truth, unless a grain of wheat falls to the ground and dies, it remains only a single seed. But if it dies, it produces many seeds. The [*wo*]man who loves [*her*] life will lose it, while the [*wo*]man who hates [*her*] life in this world will keep it for eternal life' (John 12:24–25, my italics). It is possible to effect a change on the surface without death – we can tidy up our act, give more away, cut out certain behaviours and seek to live the Christian life in our own strength. Gradually we will become disillusioned, tired and resentful that we seem to know so little of God's joy or power. Tragically, we have downgraded the Christian message into one of sin management – transformation of our actual life and character is no longer a part of the redemptive gospel we proclaim. Yet Jesus preached and lived a gospel of true transformation requiring death and resurrection – symbolised by baptism. The old woman and her life go down into the waters of baptism and die, and the new resurrected woman emerges. In fact, the loss of our lives, or the loss of control over our lives, is the necessary pre-condition of the emergence of a new life.

Jesus and women

Jesus was born into a society with a prevailing religion: patriarchy – the dominance of men over women. It was embedded into all aspects of Jewish life: work, marriage, family life, law and education. *'In Jewish law a woman had no legal rights and was the possession of first her father, and then her husband. She had no rights to divorce him, though he could divorce her. An orthodox Jew daily thanked God that he was not born a Gentile, a slave or a woman!'*[1] Jesus, who opposed 'religion' in all its forms was radical in His respectful treatment of women. Elaine Storkey writes:

> *We see a Jesus who was a friend to women, the poor, the discarded, the rejected … This Jesus cut across his society's attitudes to women, giving them dignity, value and approbation. He was not patronising and scornful, he did not ridicule and dismiss. Women were among his closest followers, supporting him financially and identifying with him fully.*[2]

From the very beginning of Matthew's Gospel a new attitude to women is signalled. Normally genealogies list only the fathers, yet Matthew specifically mentions five of Jesus' female ancestors. Tamar, who dressed as a prostitute in order to get pregnant by her father-in-law and so fulfil her duty to her dead husband. Rahab, the professional prostitute in Jericho, who hid the two spies sent by Joshua to report on the city. Ruth, the Moabitess, from a tribe cursed by God: 'No … Moabite or any of his descendants may enter the assembly of the LORD, even down to the tenth generation' (Deut. 23:3). Bathsheba, who 'had been Uriah's wife', but had been seduced by King David (who later arranged for her husband to be killed). Finally Mary, Jesus' mother, a teenage virgin, betrothed to Joseph, a carpenter. Many of us would have preferred to keep some of these family skeletons safely in the closet. Matthew, however, uses them to signal that with the coming of Jesus and His kingdom, racial, social and sexist barriers, as well as those caused by our sinful selfish natures, will be broken down.

An example of this is given in John chapter 8, where a woman 'caught in the act of adultery' is brought before Jesus, the crowd wanting to stone her to death. Where is the man, also complicit in the act of adultery? Is he not also to suffer the same penalty? No, not in a society where the prevailing religion is patriarchy. With the crowd demanding that the sentence of the law be carried out, Jesus reminds them of the requirement for two witnesses. (Under Jewish law you were disqualified as a witness if you had committed the same sin as the accused.) Not one of the men present (other than Jesus) is a qualified witness. Gently, lovingly, Jesus says, 'Then neither do I condemn you. Go now and leave your life of sin' (John 8:11).

When we know the truth of the following: that the true penalty for our sin is death, but the intervention of Jesus means that '… there is now no condemnation' (Rom. 8:1), our response is love, thankfulness and an obligation to live as redeemed people. 'We know that we have come to know him if we obey his commands. The man who says, "I know him," but does not do what he commands is a liar, and the truth is not in him. But if anyone obeys his word, God's love is truly made complete in him. This is how we know we are in him: Whoever claims to live in him must walk as Jesus did' (1 John 2:3–6).

We do not do this in our own strength. Charles Price, in his book, *Alive in Christ*, tells of how Christ enables us to live as redeemed people by turning commands into promises.

> *… a man … was converted to Christ while serving a prison sentence. He was in prison for stealing. During this time, someone had come and introduced him to Christ, and he was born again of the Holy Spirit. Upon his release from prison the first thing he wanted to do was to visit a church. Not knowing which to attend, he picked one at random … and sat on the back row. He looked up to the front, and to his dismay, located on two plaques either side of the pulpit were written the Ten Commandments. There were five down one side and five down the other. He thought to himself, 'That is the last thing I want to see. I know my weakness. I know my failure. The last thing I want to do is sit here and read these laws that only condemn me.' But he did read them, and as he did so he realised he was reading them very differently.*
>
> *Previously he had read 'You shall not steal', and it was a command! This time it read 'You shall not steal,' and it was a promise, as a father might say to a child he is holding, 'You will not fall'. It is not a command of the father to the child, but his promise to the child. It is he who will prevent the fall. He responded to God, 'Thank you, Lord, but why?' 'Because I have put my Spirit in you and will move you to follow my decrees and keep my laws.'[3]*

Healing the wounds

Every woman carries within her a wounded heart; and her story of life in a fallen world, among fallen people. Some have been abused verbally, sexually, emotionally or spiritually; others abandoned through the death of parents – or their emotional or physical absence. Most of us have absorbed messages of conditional acceptance based on looks, achievement or people-pleasing.

Deep down we all want to know: 'Will you love me for who I really am?' The way this question has been answered in our lives, or the strategies we've adopted to get it answered, have caused many wounds. Some are hidden in a plaster cast of control and invulnerability; others are open and bleeding in desperate neediness.

How does Jesus heal our wounds? Like a father with a young child who has grazed her knee. First He holds us and lets us cry out our tears and tell Him how painful it is. Sometimes our hurts are buried so deep we no longer feel them – we need help and a safe place in which to allow them to surface. Then, He gently and lovingly cleans the wound of all dirt: bitterness, rage, anger, slander, malice and unforgiveness (Eph. 4:31–32) – but only with our willing agreement.

After cleaning a child's wound, a parent will put a protective bandage over it to guard it from infection or further hurt. It's important that we seek God's protection and do not adopt self-protective strategies. Self-protection leads to a hardened, unresponsive heart. To love is to be vulnerable. So how are we to keep our hearts open and responsive without having our vulnerability trampled underfoot through the carelessness, selfishness or cruelty of others? We seek God's protection and His wisdom.

'Because [*she*] loves me,' says the Lord, 'I will rescue [*her*];

I will protect [*her*], for [*she*] acknowledges my name' (Psa. 91:14, my italics). Sometimes I've been unaware of my need for protection – the wounding comes out of the blue. The pain I experienced as a family member verbally attacked me in a recent email message was almost physical. Before replying I sought God's wisdom and consulted a godly friend. The temptation to hit back with the weapons of self-protection (in my case, logic and sarcasm) was almost overwhelming, but God spoke: 'These are not my weapons, Beverley – my weapons are blessing and forgiveness.' (Luke 6:28: 'Bless those who curse you …') Weak weapons in the world's eyes – but they contain the very power of the resurrection! 'For though we live in the world, we do not wage war as the world does. The weapons we fight with are not the weapons of this world. On the contrary, they have divine power to demolish strongholds. We demolish arguments and every pretension that sets itself up against the knowledge of God, and we take captive every thought to make it obedient to Christ' (2 Cor. 10:3–5).

Forgiving those that have wounded you is hard. Only in crying out my tears and acknowledging the hurt, am I ready to do the work of forgiveness. I then write the name of the person I need to forgive at the top of a sheet of paper, and note down all I hold against them: sins of commission or omission and the effects that their actions/words have had. I pray, releasing them from my judgment, and finally I destroy the sheet. It is only as I have cleaned out the dirt of unforgiveness that my wound can be healed.

Many of us have wounds that have caused us to bleed inside for years, leaving us, like the woman in Mark 5 (vv.25–34), worn out and isolated. It took great courage for her to push through the crowds and touch Jesus. Yet her wounding drove her to Him. Dare we risk letting down our defences, reaching out to Jesus, and allowing our wounded hearts to be healed? Let the words of Jesus encourage you: 'Daughter, your faith has healed you. Go in peace and be freed from your suffering' (Mark 5:34).

A new heart

The result of this amazing work of redemption is a new heart! Instead of some patched-up, scarred heart that limps along, God gives us a brand-new heart. The calloused, unresponsive heart will be removed in a total heart transplant and a new heart of flesh given to us.

> I will sprinkle clean water on you, and you will be clean; I will cleanse you from all your impurities and from all your idols. I will give you a new heart and put a new spirit in you; I will remove from you your heart of stone and give you a heart of flesh. And I will put my Spirit in you and move you to follow my decrees and be careful to keep my laws.
>
> (Ezek. 36:25–27)

What are the characteristics of this new heart?
1. A heart of flesh – it is pliable, teachable and responsive to God.
2. A heart moved to follow God's decrees – with God's law written upon it, it has renounced self-determination and can say 'Jesus is Lord'. A heart whose love for God is shown in obedience: 'If you love me, you will obey what I command' (John 14:15).
3. A cleansed heart – purified from all idols, it is no longer divided between worship of God and worship of false gods (control, possessions, beauty, health, sex, or even 'family').

4. A heart that reflects a 'change of mind' – it has renounced the evil ways and wicked deeds of the past.
5. A full heart – it knows blessing and provision: '…you will no longer suffer disgrace among the nations because of famine' (Ezek. 36:30).

But for each of us reading this, it is something more – it is a woman's heart: a heart with uniquely feminine desires. A heart whose deep question: 'Will you love me for who I really am?' has heard God's answer: 'Yes, and I always have loved you and do love you – passionately.' A heart that was designed to respond to God's love initiative and has been wooed and won by Him. God longs for us to turn to Him with a heart of passion, not duty. The word '*proskuneo*' translated 'worship' literally means 'towards' *(pros)* and 'kiss' *(kuneo)*. When we worship God we come towards Him and kiss Him.

Over the years, God has increasingly freed me to respond to His love with passion, and to expect to be romanced by my heavenly husband. Last year, in the week before Valentine's Day, I asked Him for a Valentine's card. I was very specific: I wanted it to be from Him and not 'complicated' by coming from someone else. I had no idea how He might do this, but nothing is impossible for God. On Saturday 12 February, I was speaking at a women's event at Lee Abbey and decided to stay on with a good friend for the weekend. On the Sunday evening, one of the pastoral team, Matt, was leading the service. Part-way through, he came round and gave us each a Valentine's card from God! Never before had I been in a service where this had happened, but then never before had I asked God for a Valentine's card! I knew that God had placed a desire in my heart to be romanced by Him and had provided a channel for that to happen. My Valentine's card read:

I'm never going to stop loving you (Jer. 31:3). If I collected up all the times I think about you, they would fill the beach at Woolacombe (Psa. 139:17–18). I make up happy songs about you and sing them in the shower (Zeph. 3:17). I'm your biggest fan (2 Thess. 2:16–17). So you just try and stop me from doing good things for you (Jer. 32:40). After all you are the most valuable thing that I've got (Exod. 19:5). You know I'll be there whenever it hurts (Psa. 34:18). You can cry on my shoulder forever (Rev. 21:3–4). I have given up so much so we could be together (2 Cor. 5:18–19). I went bankrupt just to gain your affection and I want you to know that nothing can ever come between us (Rom. 8:38–39). Come home with me now and I'll throw the most extravagant party you ever did see! (Luke 15:7). You really have stolen my heart with that twinkle in your eye and that beautiful fragrance on your skin (Songs 4:9–10). My darling, you are lovely, so very lovely (Songs 4:1).[4]

Our hearts are designed for love – they are fashioned not just to walk by God's side, but to dance in His arms! I love to dance. One day I sensed the Lord was saying to me: 'I no longer want to jive with you, I want to waltz.' The jive is a fast dance with lots of movement, yet the couple usually stay on the same spot on the dance floor. The contact between them is constantly changing: sometimes a ballroom hold, sometimes a hand hold and, when pushed into a spin, briefly there is no physical contact. The waltz, on the other hand, requires much more bodily contact – so much so that when it was first introduced into English society it was considered improper for 'respectable' young ladies to dance it without permission. Although a gentler flowing dance, the couple move right around the ballroom. The woman only sees where she has been, not where she is going. She is required to trust her partner completely – allowing him to guide her and knowing that if he pauses it's to protect her from harm. Her role is to keep in time and to follow. She is then totally free to enjoy the dance, as she yields herself fully to her partner's lead.

Jesus invites us, as redeemed women with responsive hearts of flesh, to dance into life – will you accept?

For reflection

• In what areas do you struggle with letting go of 'self-rule'?

• Jesus' attitude to women was radically different from that of society. Spend time allowing Him to show you how He views you and your role.

• Where in your life have you settled for 'sin management', instead of asking for transformation?

• Ask the Lord to show you any situations or past events where forgiveness is needed.

• Are there any wounds that still have the dirt of bitterness, anger, malice or resentment infecting them?

• Imagine yourself dancing with Jesus. What dance are you doing? How do you feel?

Chapter 4

Chosen

'My lover spoke and said to me, "Arise, my darling,
my beautiful one, and come with me."'
Song of Songs 2:10

Our homegroup meeting had been particularly enjoyable that evening. A rich discussion and Bible study on John 15 had blessed us all. Peter, who was leading the study, asked us each to share some part of the passage that was particularly meaningful to us. May, a new Christian with no church background, had been understandably quiet for most of the evening, content to listen and reflect. When Peter asked her to share, her face glowed as she exclaimed, 'I'd never realised that He chose me!' Pointing to verse 16, 'You did not choose me, but I chose you …', she told us that she'd thought that the decision to belong to Christ had been hers. Now she realised that Jesus had taken the initiative. The knowledge of her 'being chosen' radiated from her face.

In the first three chapters of Mark's Gospel we see, again and again, Jesus calling people to Himself: 'Come, follow me.' It is a call into relationship – to be with Him: 'Jesus went up on a mountainside and called to him those he wanted, and they came to him. He appointed twelve – designating them apostles – that they might be with him …' (Mark 3:13–14). It's a relationship that changes everything: our attitudes, our work, our other relationships, our hopes and our destiny.

Calling is the truth that God calls us to himself so decisively that everything we are, everything we do, and everything we have is invested with a special devotion, dynamism, and direction lived out as a response to his summons and service.[1]

… in order to live a spiritual life, we have to claim for ourselves that we are 'taken' or 'chosen'… When I know that I am chosen, I know that I have been seen as a special person. Someone has noticed me in my uniqueness and has expressed a desire to know me, to come closer to me, to love me.[2]

'Arise'

One day, Jesus whispered to my spirit: 'Arise, my darling, my beautiful one, and come with me' (Songs 2:10). As I meditated on this, my focus kept being drawn to the word, 'Arise'. I searched the commentaries, trying to understand what Jesus was saying to me. Then I found it – the sentence leapt off the page at me: 'Arise' – meaning 'come back to life.' This was why Jesus had come: to call us back to life. Not back to life in Eden – the garden is now guarded by cherubim and a flaming sword (Gen. 3:24) – but to give us back His life and restore His image in us.

Why did Jesus need to call me back to life? A medical checkup would have quickly revealed that all my vital organs were functioning well; my general health was good. I had an enjoyable and interesting job and many good friends. My relationship with Jesus was growing and deepening, so where was the lack of life? Six years before, my husband had left and we divorced. The experience was so painful that, without articulating it, I had decided that I would never be hurt like that again. In order to guarantee this I had anaesthetised my heart: this medically healthy organ could no longer feel the depths of pain, nor the heights of joy – I was safe. And yet this whisper persisted: 'Come back to life, come back to life …' I asked the Lord to show me what was going on in my heart and how the divorce had affected me. As He showed me, I wrote the following in my journal:

Divorce: *Our marriage is handed to the solicitors and left to die*
Lots are cast for our belongings and money divided between us
People stare or gloat, saying knowingly that they had expected it.
This is divorce.

Divorce: *I walk through the ordinariness of life*
But my very being is out of joint and my heart melted within me.
I am wounded deeply and my strength has dried up
– Poured out in a pretence of normality.
This is divorce.

Divorce: *My tomb has been of my choosing*
The protective rock feels so safe
My cold flesh, an anaesthetic against pain
The darkness, a cover for my woundedness and shame
The stone, my defence against life.

Lord: *You stand outside my tomb*
You shake with anger at my torment
You weep with grief at my pain and loss
You order the stone to be rolled away.

Light enters the darkness and I am afraid – vulnerable.
I cower in a corner – can I face the crowd?
You command me to come out and my feet obey, yet I tremble.
Gentle hands remove my grave clothes – gone are my defences.
I am 'let go' from all that bound me.

What now, O Lord?
I stand before You torn – torn between the longing for the safety of my tomb
And the delicious feeling of the sun, the fresh air – of life itself.
I cannot go back, for I am alive again!
I cannot choose darkness when You are in the light.
And so I walk away from my empty tomb
I put my hand in Yours and choose life.

As I put my hand in His, He led me back to the times of pain and gave me the strength to face them and receive His healing. I struggled with the passage in James: 'Consider it pure joy, my brothers, whenever you face trials of many kinds …' (1:2). My scientific background told me that 'pure' meant uncontaminated – nothing but joy would result. It didn't make sense. Then, whilst at Lee Abbey, I was listening to a talk by Gay Perry on joy. She explained that sorrow and suffering hollow out a well within us that fills with tears. Deep wells produce pure water. As the tears are cried out, this well becomes our capacity for joy. Some while later, during a meal with a friend, I was telling her about an evening class I'd joined. I was joking about some of the content when I caught a tearful look on her face. I enquired as to what the matter was. 'Bev, they are tears of thankfulness – I'd begun to think that I would never hear you laugh again.' On a recent holiday, one of the men paid me a great compliment: 'I always know which table you are on at meal times – it's where the laughter is!' Is my capacity for joy greater because of sorrow? I believe so.

When God calls us into relationship He is not looking for cold intellectual assent to a set of beliefs, nor an attitude of duty that compels us to perform a variety of good deeds. No, He is looking for a passionate love relationship that will transform our lives – and for that we need hearts that are fully alive; hearts that have the capacity for joy.

Beloved

'Arise, my darling, my beautiful one, and come with me' (Songs 2:10). God calls us to become His beloved, His darling, His beautiful one and, in doing so, He bestows on us a new identity.

'Whose young woman is that?'(Ruth 2:5). This question,

posed by Boaz to his foreman, elicits an interesting response. The foreman proceeds to define Ruth in terms of her ethnicity: 'She is the Moabitess'; her relationships: 'with Naomi'; and her work: 'She went into the field and has worked steadily from morning till now …' (vv.6–7).

Like Ruth, our identity is both formed and expressed in a variety of ways: our relationships, roles, ethnicity, possessions, marital status, clothing, life circumstances, hopes and aspirations. Yet, at its very core, I believe that the essence of our identity is a gift from God – a gift received at the moment of conception. He designed me – shaped me in my mother's womb. My identity can only be fully realised when I am reborn in Christ – when I accept the new life He offers through His death and resurrection.

The Father's voice speaks my new identity into being: 'You are My Beloved, on you My favour rests.' Being the Beloved expresses the core truth of our existence.

From the moment we claim the truth of being the Beloved, we are faced with the call to become who we are … Becoming the Beloved means letting the truth of our Belovedness become enfleshed in everything we think, say or do. It entails a long and painful process of appropriation or, better, incarnation. As long as 'being the Beloved' is little more than a beautiful thought or lofty idea that hangs above my life to keep me from becoming depressed, nothing really changes … Becoming the Beloved is pulling the truth revealed to me from above down into the ordinariness of what I am, in fact, thinking of, talking about, and doing from hour to hour.' [3]

When a woman marries, it is customary for her to change her surname to that of her husband. This change of name signifies a change in her identity: she is no longer an 'individual' but one half of a couple – two have become one. Scripture evidences a dynamic view of names and naming – the name given is seen as embodying the Word of God, which will mould its recipient into the man or woman described by the name. For example, Sarai becomes Sarah, 'mother of nations', and Jacob becomes Israel, 'he struggles with God'. Similarly in the New Testament, Simon becomes Peter, 'the Rock' and Saul becomes Paul. When we are redeemed by Christ we get a new name: Christian. Luke places the first use of this name meaning 'of the household of Christ' at Antioch in Syria (Acts 11:26). At baptism we are given our 'Christian' name. We are now identified with Christ. He is in us and we are in Him.

This new identity of being 'in Christ' transcends our identity as women. It 'defines' us in a way that no other statement about us can – not our ethnicity, our role, our marital status nor even our gender. 'You are all sons of God through faith in Christ Jesus, for all of you who were baptised into Christ have clothed yourselves with Christ. There is neither Jew nor Greek, slave nor free, male nor female, for you are all one in Christ Jesus' (Gal. 3:26–28).

Abiding

What does it mean for us to be 'in Christ' and for Him to be 'in us'? Jesus uses a picture of the vine to illustrate this truth. 'Remain [abide] in me, and I will remain [abide] in you' (John 15:4). Andrew Murray writes:

> When a new graft is placed in a vine, and it abides there, there is a twofold process that takes place. The first is in the wood. The graft shoots its little roots and fibers down into the stem, and the stem

grows up into the graft, and what has been called the structural union is effected. The graft abides and becomes one with the vine, and even though the vine were to die, would still be one wood with it. Then there is the second process, in which the sap of the vine enters the new structure, and uses it as a passage through which sap can flow up to show itself in young shoots and leaves and fruit. Here is the vital union. Into the graft which abides in the stock, the stock enters with sap to abide in it.[4]

As I have studied these words, the questions of 'How do I remain?' and 'What must I do to abide?' have puzzled me. I've wanted a ten-point plan with guaranteed outcomes. Yet to 'work' at 'abiding', to 'strive' to 'rest' are paradoxes – sometimes it does require us to make deliberate choices to be able to 'abide in God'. 'Abiding' denotes complete dependency and trust, plus a level of intimacy that can only come through 'time together' and communication. Many of us shy away from extended time with God, not quite knowing what is expected of us or 'how to do it'. Alternatively, we approach God with a full agenda of prayer requests. Romans 8:26–27 makes it clear that God does not expect us to know how to pray – we need the Holy Spirit's help. Our responsibility is to keep the appointment: how the meeting goes is God's responsibility, providing we allow the Holy Spirit to chair it! Over time, as you and I allow His Spirit to work in us, we will find a growing level of anticipation as we approach this time. So do not give up, for if the very reason for my existence and the source of my identity is to be found 'in Christ', I cannot, must not, dare not give up on time with Him!

So, is there a strategy – a ten-point plan? The old chorus is as good a strategy to abiding as you will find:

Trust and obey
For there's no other way
To be happy in Jesus
But to trust and obey![5]

Trust and obey

'*To trust the real person Jesus is to have confidence in him in every dimension of our real life, to believe that he is right about and adequate to everything.*'[6] The belief that many of us act out, whatever our mouths profess, is that God, His wisdom, His strength and His life are irrelevant to our day-to-day lives. '*It is left unexplained how it is that one can rely on Christ for the next life without doing so for this one, trust him for one's eternal destiny without trusting him for "the things that relate to Christian life." Is this really possible? Surely it is not! Not within one life.*'[7]

Trust grows. Gradually I learn to confront those things in which I have been taught to trust that are not Christ. As I seek to trust Him in every aspect of my life: my health, finances, problems, work, family, friendships and future, so trust grows. I even learn to trust Christ when under attack. For me, learning to trust has meant challenging both 'self-reliance' and 'self-protection', and then asking God to show me when I am slipping back into old patterns. Beth Clark, part of the CWR Women's Ministry Team until 2006, and my friend, encourager and mentor, says that we need to learn to 'lie flat on the promises of God' – a picture of true rest.

My baptismal verse is Proverbs 3:5: 'Trust in the LORD with all your heart and lean not on your own understanding'. My temptation is always to lean on my own understanding. I spend much wasted time and effort trying to understand what the Lord is doing or asking Him to explain 'Why?' before I obey. In

His graciousness He leads me into more and more situations that just do not make sense. Every time, I am confronted with the choice to obey without understanding or to refuse to trust: to walk by faith or by sight.

What exactly does it mean to trust? It means that I trust Jesus' character, His competence, His commitment and His communication. Failure to trust may be traced back to one or more of these areas, and it is often helpful to identify which.

His character

Do I believe that Jesus is good, for no other reason than that He says He is? My belief in His goodness is not dependent on whether the sun is shining, whether things are going well, or I feel on top of the world. Do I trust His goodness even in the valley of the shadow of death, when all light seems extinguished and all hope gone?

His competence

Is Jesus able to do what He says? Do I truly believe that 'nothing is impossible with God'; that He is able to deal with my situation, illness, problems and so on?

His commitment

Is He willing to use His power on my behalf? Is His desire to bless *me*? Does He love me and believe in me? Will He be faithful to me even though I break faith with Him or get things wrong?

His communication

Do I believe that His sheep will know His voice? That I will hear a voice behind me saying, 'This is the way; walk in it' (Isa. 30:21)? Do I trust that Jesus wants to communicate with me?

If I trust His character, competence, commitment and communication I will find myself drawn to spend time with Him. If I have greater trust in my own ability, understanding or activity then I won't! My beliefs are evidenced by what I do. Failure to spend time with God can usually be traced back to a flawed belief in the value of time spent with God – which in turn can be traced to a flawed belief or lack of trust in God Himself. Henri Nouwen expresses this so well:

> … *when I go to a quiet place to pray, I realize that, although I have a tendency to say many things to God, the real 'work' of prayer is to become silent and listen to the voice that says good things about me. This might sound self-indulgent, but, in practice, it is a hard discipline. I am so afraid of being cursed, of hearing that I am no good or not good enough, that I quickly give in to the temptation to start talking and to keep talking to control my fears. To gently push aside and silence the many voices that question my goodness and to trust that I will hear a voice of blessing … that demands real effort.*[8]

Fruitfulness

This intimacy is not an end in itself. '… I chose you and appointed you to go and bear fruit – fruit that will last' (John 15:16). Just as the intimacy and union of Adam and Eve resulted in the fruitfulness of children: 'God blessed them and said to them, "Be fruitful and increase in number"' (Gen. 1:28), so our intimacy and union with Christ is designed to bear fruit. If Adam and Eve had set up camp at opposite ends of the Garden of Eden, and had rarely communicated with each other apart from a hurried 'Good morning' and the skim-read of an occasional letter, you can be assured that there would have been no 'fruit'! Just so with us: lack of intimacy will evidence itself in lack of fruit. However hard we may be working *for Christ*, lack of intimacy *with Christ* will mean that the fruit of our labours will not last.

There is a difference in the Christian life between work and fruit. *'A machine can do work: only life can bear fruit. A law can compel work: only love can spontaneously bring forth fruit. Work implies effort and labour: the essential idea of fruit is that it is the silent natural restful produce of our inner life.'*[9]

God's desire for us is 'much fruit'. Paul's prayer for the Colossians is that they will bear fruit in every good work (Col. 1:10). Abiding is not an optional extra in the process of fruit-bearing – it is indispensable. A deep conviction of the truth of this lies at the very root of a strong spiritual life. In the next chapter we explore what 'fruit' might be evidenced as we seek to live as godly women.

'Apart from me you can do nothing'

How do we live as 'the Beloved' – the woman God has designed us to be? We cannot! No amount of effort or striving can produce God's image in us. Just as the dust of the ground could not become a man through its own efforts, so we cannot become a woman in the image of God through hard work. It is only as God forms us and breathes His life into us that we will become a 'living' woman.

Did you realise that even Jesus could do nothing through His own efforts: 'Rather, it is the Father living in me, who is doing his work' (John 14:10). If this was true for Jesus, how much more so for us? Apart from God we can do nothing – it is God's breath, His Spirit, in us that does the work of reproducing the character of Jesus in us, of changing us into

His likeness and of restoring God's image. Does that mean we have no role in this transformation, that we are passive? No, it doesn't! We can either co-operate with God's Spirit or grieve Him; we can either respond to Him or quench Him. We grieve the Holy Spirit when we fail to allow Him to do that for which He was given to us. The Spirit of Jesus has come to bring us life in all its fullness and whenever we choose those things that deaden us, we grieve Him. He can also be quenched. Every time the Spirit whispers, 'This is the way, walk in it' (Isa. 30:21), we are faced with a choice – to walk God's way or to go our own way. Sadly, consistently ignoring the Spirit's promptings will lead to increasing deafness. We will no longer hear His voice, so quenching His activity in our lives.

Do you and I want to be the women God has created us to be? Then know that you have been chosen and listen to His call – His call into relationship, His call back to life, His call to a new identity, His call to abide and His call to bear fruit. Just as a branch abides in a tree, it is our total dependence on Him and willingness to abide in Him that enables us to bear much fruit.

One of my spiritual heroes, Hudson Taylor, whose life was one of immense fruitfulness and whom God called to be a pioneer missionary in China, wrote this in a letter to his sister:

The sweetest part … is the rest which full identification with Christ brings. I am no longer anxious about anything, as I realise this; for He, I know, is able to carry out His will, and His will is mine. It makes no matter where He places me, or how. That is rather for Him to consider than for me; for in the easiest position He must give me His grace, and in the most difficult His grace is sufficient. It matters little to my servant whether I send him to buy a few cash worth of things, or the most expensive articles. In either case he looks to me for the money and brings me his purchases. So, if God should place me in serious perplexity, must He not give me much guidance; in positions of great difficulty, much grace; in circumstances of great pressure and trial, much strength? No fear that resources will prove unequal to the emergency! And His resources are mine, for He is mine, and is with me and dwells in me.[10]

As we learn to draw all we need from Him – from the Vine – then our relationships with others are transformed. I am free to bless without demanding that you bless me in return. I can allow you to be who God created you to be without trying to change you into a person who would better meet my needs. I can become more responsive to the transformational work God is doing in me, because I am no longer desperately seeking the approval of others. As I hear, in that quiet place, the truth of my belovedness, I know a greater and greater freedom *not* to dance to the world's tune but to keep time with the heartbeat of God. I discover that I am alive!

For reflection:

- You have been chosen by God for relationship with Him. How does this thought affect you day to day?

- Is there any life experience that has caused you to deaden your heart?

- Spending time with God can take many different forms – what does this mean for you?

- Are there situations in your life where you are tempted to lean on your own understanding?

- Where you are aware of a lack of trust, is this a lack of trust in His character, His competence, His commitment or His communication?

- Ask God to encourage you by showing you the areas where His life in you is producing fruit.

Chapter 5

Woman transformed

And we, who with unveiled faces all reflect
the Lord's glory, are being transformed into his
likeness with ever-increasing glory, which comes
from the Lord, who is the Spirit.
2 Corinthians 3:18

We are all on a journey – the journey of becoming the women God created us to be. It's a journey of constant transformation. Each of our journeys is different, reflecting our differing life circumstances and callings – there is no road map with a definitive route clearly marked that is the only way. As a young believer, coming from a non-Christian family, I was desperate to learn. I devoured books by amazing Christian women like Catherine Marshall, Evelyn Christenson, Hannah Hurnard and others. These women became my spiritual mothers, nurturing me in the faith. Their journey was not to be mine, but lessons and principles from their lives guided and informed my own path. My debt of gratitude to them is immense. In this chapter I have sought to offer some aspects of my own journey, not as a blueprint for yours, but as 'helps' along the way.

Lord, change me!

This was the title of one of the first of Evelyn Christenson's books that I read. She openly shared about the joys and trials of family life and the temptation to pray 'Lord, change them!' One day the Lord confronted her: if she wanted her prayers answered then she would need to change them to 'Lord, change me!' This is not something that happens overnight. Deep down I like to believe that I am right and others wrong; that others need to change and I don't. Yet the Lord longs to transform us and will use all the circumstances of our lives in that process: every piece of grit can be transformed by Him into a pearl. How does He do this? By teaching us to pray: 'Search me, O God, and know my heart; test me and know my anxious thoughts. See if there is any offensive way in me, and lead me in the way everlasting' (Psa. 139:23–24).

The Lord has the power to change any and every circumstance of our lives, but His first priority is our personal transformation. That transformation may be the courage to lovingly confront or leave wrong or abusive situations.

Do you want to be changed? All change is difficult – it involves moving out of our comfort zones, risking failure and daring to do things differently, to live differently. For Jesus, hearing God's Word always implied obedience to God. The great Danish philosopher, Søren Kierkegaard, provocatively challenges our lack of obedience:

> *The matter is quite simple. The Bible is very easy to understand. But we Christians are a bunch of scheming swindlers. We pretend to be unable to understand it because we know very well that the minute we understand we are obliged to act accordingly. Take any words in the New Testament and forget everything except pledging yourself to act accordingly. My God, you will say, if I do that my whole life will be ruined. How would I ever get on in the world? ... Dreadful it is to fall into the hands of the living God. Yes, it is even dreadful to be alone with the New Testament.* [1]

Sadly, it is only as the pain of staying the same has become too great, or my circumstances too painful, that I have willingly submitted to being changed. At one point I pictured my life as a smashed earthenware pot – the broken pieces being lovingly collected together by Jesus. 'Did it have to be broken?' I asked. 'Yes,' was His tender reply, 'it was the only way I could remake it.' More recently I was celebrating a significant birthday and God again gave me a word about remodelling a clay pot. Fearfully I wondered what would have to be smashed. The picture of the potter and the clay came to mind and I knew that when the clay was wet and pliable it was only the pressure of the potter's hands that was needed to remake it and fashion it for new purposes.

Living as godly women is not, primarily, a set of rules to be followed or disciplines to be observed, it is first and foremost a romance: I am my Beloved's and He is mine. And so, as with any love relationship, we long to read His love letters to us; we are eager to talk through our day with Him and receive His wisdom; we love being held by Him when we are hurt or tired, resting in the security of His embrace. We allow that love to change us.

A woman who laughs

> She is clothed with strength and dignity; she can laugh at the days to come.
>
> (Prov. 31:25)

Proverbs 31 is one of my favourite chapters of the Bible. Many women find this a difficult passage. The woman in Proverbs 31 has been used to support a number of conflicting viewpoints. She has been used to advocate the career woman and held up as the working woman's model. She has been used as an example for the stay-at-home woman (who also works). It would seem that most women's reaction to Proverbs 31 is one of discouragement. Here is 'Superwoman' – an impossible role model whom I can't live up to.

Let me encourage you to come to this passage afresh and to see what God would say to us through it. The context is that of a mother giving advice to her son – King Lemuel. Her advice is that to be a successful king there are two things he needs to avoid. Firstly, he must avoid drunkenness; and secondly, choosing the wrong wife, because she would sap his strength and prevent him from being the leader God has called him to be. Also, this woman lived in a pre-industrial era, which meant that work and home, for both men and women, went hand in hand. The hard choice between staying at home or 'going out' to work, faced by many women today, was not hers.

We can feel daunted by this woman who seems to achieve so much with her day. What attracts me to her however is that, despite her activity, she is a woman at rest. Her work and relationships flow from a heart at rest. She is a woman who fears the Lord and so can laugh at the days to come. She is clothed with strength and dignity.

Why is she able to laugh at the future? It is not that she has her life totally under control and relies on the millions stashed away in her bank account. Her laughter springs from the security that her life is in God's hands and she can entrust all her tomorrows into His care. This is what it means to fear God – to trust totally in His control, His goodness and His covenant love.

I had the privilege of attending a conference at which Rolland and Heidi Baker were speaking. Sitting, literally, at Heidi's feet as she spoke, her laughter bubbled up like a brook. Working in one of the poorest, most war-torn countries in the world, Mozambique, God has used Rolland, Heidi and their organisation, Iris Ministries, to feed the poor. (On a normal day they feed 6,000 children, but during the floods this number escalates many times.) They are also used in caring for the orphans, placing them in families, and have been involved in planting 6,000 churches, as thousands of Muslims turn to Christ. With responsibilities that would daunt the strongest of us, how can Heidi laugh? Because she believes and lives out the truth that, in God, 'there is always enough'. Her prayer letter of March 2007 evidences this:

We are overwhelmed with gratitude for people who have been helping us 'for such a time as this'. The Lord spoke to me from John 6 that Iris Ministries is an example of the boy with his bread and fish. We have handed Jesus our lunch and He is multiplying it for the multitudes. Tens of thousands of people have given their hearts to Jesus in these last weeks! The deaf have heard, the blind have seen and the poor have heard the Good News. I don't think I have ever seen such suffering and hunger as I encountered in the camps in Zambezia. We thank God every day for your love and concern for the poor.

Being a woman who laughs does not mean that your life will be free of heartache. Ruth is the other biblical woman of whom the word 'noble' is used (Ruth 3:11) and she experiences bereavement, poverty and the hardships of living in a foreign country. Yet her response is to take refuge under the wings of the Lord, the God of Israel (Ruth 2:12).

Have you ever spent time with women who are not at rest? Five minutes with them and you feel the need to lie down for an hour! Their busy, fearful hearts are 'worried and upset about many things' and demand that your heart carry the same burdens (Luke 10:38–42), instead of allowing you to sit quietly at the Lord's feet, listening to His words.

A woman who fears God can invite you into the home of her presence. There your heart will delight in the richest of fare – treasures stored up from her times alone with God – and you will experience refreshment and restoration. With her, you can learn to laugh again, even in the midst of pain.

A woman who brings good

She brings him good, not harm, all the days of her life.

(Prov. 31:12)

A key characteristic of the godly woman of Proverbs is that she brings good, not harm, to all her relationships, both near and far: her husband, her children, her servant girls, those she trades with, and the poor and needy. This is Eve redeemed – instead of offering Adam the fruit of the knowledge of good and evil, she offers him the fruit of the Spirit.

How does she do this? We know that her heart fears the Lord, but how is this trust in God translated into good for others? Notice in Proverbs 31 the emphasis on other parts of her body: eager hands (vv.13,19) which are extended to the needy (v.20); her arms are strong (v.17) and open to the poor (v.20); her fingers work (v.19); and faithful instruction is on her tongue (v.26). We bring good, not just through our fear of God, but by translating that trust into action – by obeying what He tells us to do. Trust and obedience go hand in hand. If we seek to obey God's commands without a corresponding trust in Him for the strength and ability those commands require, we will find ourselves frustrated and discouraged. Conversely, a trust in God that doesn't manifest itself in active obedience leads to passive mysticism. *'The foundation of a life of faith is obedience. Move outside of an obedience to the will of God and you move outside of the resources of God. They simply dry up.'*[2]

The key to 'bringing good' is, I believe, a heart attitude of generosity. It is hard to be generous when I do not fully trust in God's provision and protection – when I believe that my best guarantee of a secure future is a 'healthy' bank balance. This is an area of real challenge for me, and one of my 'growing edges'.

'So when you give to the needy …' (Matt. 6:2–3) – here Jesus assumes that His followers will be generous. Brian McLaren expands this point:

> … *giving to the poor begins Jesus' list of spiritual practices: if we are to experience spiritual transformation so that we can become the kinds of people whose 'righteousness' transcends the mere avoidance of doing wrong, mere technical perfection and external conformity – then we must be liberated from enslavement to money … Money, it turns out, is a cruel task-master; when you serve money, soon you will resent God for interfering with your humming, expanding economic kingdom.*[3]

God is also challenging me to be generous with my time. Sometimes the easy option is to write the cheque – it's much harder to give away our minutes and hours. Twice, while writing this book, I have known this challenge. Days that have been earmarked for writing He has asked me to give away. I did so, trusting that I had heard correctly, and yet unsure as to how I would meet my deadline. In just the last week, three days of courses have been postponed until after my writing deadline – giving me the much-needed time! It's a slow lesson, but I am gradually glimpsing the truth that we never lose when we give, in obedience to God.

Notice, in Proverbs 31, all the very practical results of this woman's fear of the Lord: her husband and children are blessed, her household is well run, her trading profitable, her hospitality warm, her speech wise and she is generous to the poor. No pampered woman of leisure – she is a woman who is active in bringing good to others.

Called to be life-bearers

You will be with child and give birth to a son, and … give him the name Jesus.'

(Luke 1:31)

Just as Eve became 'the mother of all the living' so we, her redeemed daughters, are called to bring forth spiritual life. Mary was chosen to 'be with child and give birth to a son …' She was called to physically carry Jesus into the world. We too have His life in us and are called to carry Him into our world. I was once told that, on average, a person's world consists of about seventeen people – the people we have ongoing relationships with at home, at work and socially. Imagine the impact if every redeemed woman took seriously the commission of Jesus to 'Go into all the world and preach the good news' (Mark 16:15) and bore witness to Jesus, through her life and words, within her circle of seventeen people.

What stops us? Fear! Imagine if Mary had responded to God's call like this: 'Lord, what would people (Joseph, my family, my village) think? I'd lose my reputation and, even if they didn't stone me to death, my life would be very uncomfortable! Surely You have someone else You could ask.' Instead, we read that her response is to glorify God, to rejoice that He has chosen her to play a part in His salvation plan for the world and to respond 'I am the Lord's servant … May it be to me as you have said' (Luke 1:38).

Women have always had a key role to play in God's salvation purposes – they are life-bearers: of His life. Who were the first people to know of His resurrection? The women! Who were the first people to whom the resurrected Jesus appeared? The women! Who were the first to be entrusted with the task of telling others of His resurrection? The women!

For those of us who work in non-Christian organisations, this is often where we have the greatest opportunity to share our faith and to bring life. One morning, as I was praying, the realisation hit me that it had been a while since I had shared my faith at work. I asked specifically for an opening to do so that day. Eager to avoid the traffic, I set off early to the training course I was running and planned to do my daily Bible study upon arrival. Others also arrived early and I was not able to have my planned study. So, instead of going for a walk at lunchtime, I stayed in the training room. One of the delegates re-entered the training room shortly after we had broken for lunch. I welcomed her, giving her the option to sit quietly or to talk. After a few minutes, she exclaimed, 'I feel as if I am just waiting to die.' No, she was not suicidal, nor was she old. She explained that if death were the end, then there seemed no real point to living. She then asked whether she was stupid for thinking in such a way. 'No one else seems to be worried by it,' she said. I told her about King Solomon, considered to be one of the wisest men ever, who had asked just the same questions and had set up a research project, detailed in the book of Ecclesiastes, to try to find some answers. His conclusion: if death is the end, then everything is meaningless – the best we can hope for is to eat, drink and be merry, for tomorrow we die. But if there is life after death and a God who judges, then all life is infused with meaning. Our conversation was part of her journey – a journey that led her to join a local church and explore Christianity. Some months later, she sent me an email entitled, 'And still it grows'.

For things to grow, they have to be alive. For them to be alive, we need to embrace with gratitude our role as life-bearers. Will you embrace your God-given role?

Trained for battle!

He trains my hands for battle; my arms can bend a bow of bronze.

(Psa. 18:34)

Are you trained for battle? God's call for all redeemed women is to take their place in the spiritual battle that is being waged in their homes, schools, workplaces, towns, churches, and nations – to be warrior princesses!

As the film was nearing its end, my sister-in-law shouted out in disgust: 'They can't do that – they've changed her character.' She was referring to Maid Marian in the film, *Robin Hood, Prince of Thieves*. In Marian's first scene she is in black leather fighting apparel, armed with a sword, challenging Robin to single combat. In the scene that had caused my sister-in-law's outcry, she is in a floaty white nightdress, leaping pathetically from window ledge to window ledge, emitting frightened 'Oohs' and 'Aaghs' as Robin fights with the sheriff. What has happened to her? Maid Marian the warrior has become a wimp!

Through my work I meet many women and I hear how much the devil is stealing from under their very noses: their marriages, their children, their health … These lovely women metaphorically don their nightdresses, kneel by their beds, ask God to do something, and then go to sleep! Wake up! God's body is His Church – He acts in and through His people. So take off your nightdress and 'put on the full armour of God so that you can take your stand against the devil's schemes' (Eph. 6:11).

Esther received her wake-up call from her uncle, Mordecai, who urged her to go to the king and plead for her people. Notice how Esther armed herself for battle: she sought prayer cover, fasted and prayed.

Make no mistake, we are all in a spiritual battle. The ultimate victory has already been secured by Christ's death on the cross but the devil still seeks to destroy all that is life-giving and good. Don't give him a foothold (Eph. 4:26–27). Many Christians unknowingly wear occult jewellery, have African death masks, Egyptian gods, Buddhas, fertility symbols, 'evil eyes' and other holiday 'souvenirs' on display in their houses – then wonder why there is no peace in their homes and illness in their lives! John Eldredge writes:

> *You won't understand your life, you won't see clearly what has happened to you or how to live forward from here, unless you see it as a* battle. *A war against your heart.*
>
> *For if [the Enemy] can disable or deaden your heart, then he has effectively foiled the plan of God, which was to create a world where love reigns. By taking out your heart, the Enemy takes out* you, *and you are essential to the Story.*[4]

God can train us for battle – ask Him to bring you into contact with more experienced prayer warriors, to show you which books to read, and to encourage you in fasting. The devil is a defeated foe, but our complacency allows him to steal much that we value. Will you wake up, discard the nightdress and put on your armour?

Marching to a different drum

The Sermon on the Mount is a revolutionary manifesto. In it Jesus spells out what it means to live counter-culturally. The pressures on us to conform to the pattern of this world are immense. The television, magazines and newspapers all pressurise us to look a certain way, to be successful, to live fulfilled lives and to focus on our own needs and enjoyment – because we 'are worth it!' In her book, *Contributions to Christian Feminism*, Elaine Storkey sketches four kinds of women, including the 'new woman'. I number many 'new women' among my friends and meet them daily on courses. What are the defining characteristics of the 'new woman'?

> ... *she is often a young, professional, able, competent woman, who, in many senses, has grown up in a different gender culture from that of her mother and certainly from that of her grandmother ... She is a woman who belongs to the culture which invites us to draw up our own agendas, and write our own scripts, including of course our own sexual scripts. So there is no impetus here to find a mate or to marry, for freedom for her is having the right to make her own decisions ... However, she is a woman caught up in activity, a busy woman who can measure out her time in half-hour slots and who is aiming to get to the top ... The new woman is post-feminist and a growing part of the individualism, activity, hierarchy, and competitiveness of the contemporary rat race ... In fact, the new woman is hardly any different from the old man.*[5]

'New woman' is just as much conformed to the norms of this world as her mother was. To live counter-culturally is not about returning to the stereotypical female role models of the past, nor to centre our world exclusively in home, family and church. Our presence is needed, even vital, in the schools, workplaces, political arenas and social gatherings of our society. To make a difference we have to see ourselves as a part of a body, not as individuals – a part of Christ's Body.

We also need to take seriously just how much we have been

'squeezed into the world's mould'. We can only begin to live counter-culturally when we do it hand in hand with our loving Saviour and in the strength of His Spirit. To pray 'Your kingdom come' means marching to the beat of a different drum. Brian McLaren, summarising the Sermon on the Mount, puts it like this:

> *The kingdom of God, then, is a revolutionary, counter-cultural movement – proclaiming a ceaseless rebellion against the tyrannical trinity of money, sex, and power. Its citizens resist the occupation of this invisible Caesar through three categories of spiritual practice. First they practice a liberating* generosity toward the poor *to dethrone greed and topple the regime of money. Second, they practice a kind of* prayer *that is a defiant act of resistance against the prideful pursuit of power, pursuing forgiveness and reconciliation, not retaliation and revenge. Finally, they practice* fasting *to revolt against the dominating impulses of physical gratification – so that the sex drive and other physical appetites will not become our slave drivers. All of these are practiced covertly,* in secret, *so they aren't corrupted into an external show 'as the hypocrites do'.*[6]

Your presence is required

A few years ago, four of us, including Mark Greene, from LICC (the London Institute for Contemporary Christianity), were invited to attend a 'Christians in the Workplace' conference being hosted by the Billy Graham organisation in the States. Over a third of the delegates were women, yet there was no woman speaker on the main platform. Also, with the wonderful exceptions of Eddie Gibbs and Mark Greene, the language used by the other speakers was exclusively male-orientated. In one of the final sessions, a panel of four of the speakers took to the platform to answer questions from the floor. One woman asked about the role of women in this whole mission. As Mark took the microphone I knew instinctively what he would do – he would invite me to join him on the platform. A slight shake of the head from me would mean that the invitation would never be verbalised. My mind went blank – what would I say if I went up there? The more mundane consideration of 'I wish I was wearing something smarter' also hovered. Yet Mark was not inviting me onto the platform to impart particular pearls of wisdom, nor was I expected to be some ornamental garnish – my presence was required. In that one invitation, Mark demonstrated more powerfully than any words could that it is only as men and women partner together in our workplaces, our churches, our families and our God-given mission that we can truly reflect the image of God. And so I nodded as Mark looked in my direction and the invitation was issued. I went onto the platform, was given the microphone, and took my place alongside the men. Why? Because my presence was required! Just as God's creation could not be complete until Eve had taken her place in the garden alongside Adam, so the ongoing redemptive story of this world requires women to take their place – not usurping the role of men, but in partnership with them.

For reflection

• •

- Reflect with thankfulness on the women who have been role models for you.

- Dare you pray 'Lord, change me'?

- Can you laugh at the days to come?

- Ask the Lord to show you what it means to 'bring good' into the different areas of your life.

- Is there anyone the Lord might be asking you to speak to about Him?

- Are you aware of the spiritual battle? What might it mean to train your hands for battle?

- Ask God to show you where you have been conformed to the pattern of this world and what it might mean to live counter-culturally.

- Where is your presence required?

Chapter 6

Woman in glory

*'Let us rejoice and be glad and give him glory!
For the wedding of the Lamb has come, and his
bride has made herself ready.'*
Revelation 19:7

What a celebration! The church was packed and extra seats had to be found. The atmosphere was joyful, the singing triumphant, the flowers glorious and the love tangible. No, this wasn't a wedding. It was the funeral of Jean Waller, a member of our church for fifty years, and now a woman in glory. Our minister explained that the hymns had been chosen by friends as Jean had no family, in the natural sense. Her husband, Tommy, had died eight years previously and they had been unable to have children. I had spoken at a Ladies' Breakfast in our church two years earlier on what it meant to be created as a woman. We had looked together at the call of all women to be mothers, life-bearers, and I had explained that this was in no way limited by singleness or infertility. Jean had come up to me afterwards, with tears in her eyes. 'I had never realised that all these years I have been a mother,' she said. Jean may not have realised, but everyone else in the church had. Our minister was forced to limit the number of tributes during the service to fifteen, though in one sense the two hundred and fifty people at the funeral were all paying their tribute. Nearly all the spoken tributes contained mention of Jean as being a part of their family: some were to 'Auntie Jean'; others 'honoured her as a mother'. They spoke of warm hospitality and an ever-open door; of generosity of time, money, flowers or cards to encourage; of a listening ear or the offer of her strength to others in their times of weakness. Most of all they spoke of her strong faith in Jesus, with whom she now was.

At funerals it is natural to focus on death and the afterlife; to wonder what heaven is like. John seeks to give us a glimpse of heaven in the last two chapters of Revelation, but language proves inadequate. Selwyn Hughes voices this realisation:

This I feel is John's predicament as he writes in these closing chapters concerning the joys and delights of heaven. He just doesn't have the words. He pushes language to its utmost limit as he focuses on trying to explain what heaven is like ... there is one thing I am certain about and it is this – however we view it, heaven is grander and greater and more glorious than any human words or descriptions can convey. [1]

Perhaps in reaction to the 'pie in the sky when you die' mentality or the dangers of a future focus that ignores Jesus' practical teaching for the 'here and now', I have often relegated thoughts of heaven to the sidelines of my Christian life. It may also be that I am too 'at home' in this world. When God made us He set eternity in our hearts (Eccl. 3:11) – a homesickness for heaven, a true nostalgia (*'nostos'* meaning 'return home' and *'algos'* meaning 'pain'). Built into our hearts is an ache for our heavenly home – an ache that we allow too easily to be dulled by the things of this life. Malcolm Muggeridge wrote: *'The only ultimate disaster that can befall us ... is to feel ourselves at home here on earth. As long as we are aliens we cannot forget our true homeland.'* [2]

It is no coincidence that the original readers of Revelation lived in constant threat of oppression from the religious authorities and the Roman Empire. It is also no coincidence that those whose focus on heaven is strongest can be found in the Persecuted Church. I was speaking to a Romanian pastor whose life had been threatened by the Secret Police because of his clear preaching of the gospel. He knew that this was a very real threat, having just conducted the funeral of a fellow pastor for whom an 'accident' had been arranged. His reply to the police was: 'You cannot threaten me with heaven!'

Paul exhorts us to set our hearts and minds on the things

above because we have died to this world and its priorities. Our life is now hidden with Christ in God (Col. 3:1–4). Yet here is the paradox: it is those that have truly died to this life and its priorities that are most available to God for His purposes in this world. As Selwyn Hughes puts it: *'My reading of Christian history has brought me to the conclusion that the Christians who did most for this world in which we live were those who thought a good deal about the next'*[3]. He develops this thought in the epilogue of his autobiography:

One of my regrets, as I draw near to the end of my journey here on earth, is that I did not tune in earlier to this longing for home that God has built into every one of us. I think it would have made my Christian walk more effective and enhanced my life in so many ways – ways which I am enjoying now but could have enjoyed much sooner. I think I was probably afraid that a preoccupation with heaven would inhibit my usefulness here on earth. I certainly preached about heaven, but I have to confess that it did not have the 'pull' it has had upon me in the past couple of decades. Living in the light of heaven need not make us less keen to help others, but it can be a constant reminder to us that the most permanent dwelling earth provides is only a tent and at any time word may come to pull up the pegs. We are indeed strangers and pilgrims here below.[4]

How then are we to 'live in the light of heaven' in a way that positively influences our lives now? Throughout Scripture the relationship of God and His Church is often depicted as that of an engaged couple – with the grand finale of Revelation (19:7–9; 21:1–27) being the marriage feast of Jesus and His bride, the Church. The Holy Spirit is our engagement ring: 'Now it is God who makes both us and you stand firm in Christ. He anointed us, set his seal of ownership on us, and put his Spirit in our hearts as a deposit, guaranteeing what is to come' (2 Cor. 1:21–22).

Two of my close girl friends got engaged recently. One couple quickly set a date for their marriage, the other, for many good reasons, have no marriage date in view and are content to be simply 'engaged'. The difference in how both couples live *now* is instructive. Engagement has changed very little, it appears to me, in the relationship of the second couple. However, in the first couple, the bride is making herself ready in preparation for her wedding day. 'For the wedding of the Lamb has come, and his bride has made herself ready' (Rev. 19:7).

Making ourselves ready

The story of the ten virgins in Matthew 25 (vv.1–13) is a story about making ourselves ready. In some ways this can seem quite a hard parable. These bridesmaids were meant to be friends and yet they are not sharing their oil. Is that how real friends would behave? It is true that there may not have been enough oil to go around as these lamps were not small. They were to light a procession, so a significant amount of oil would have been needed. To understand the wise virgins' reaction, we need to look at what the oil represents. The oil, symbolic of the Holy Spirit, represents our preparation – our preparedness for the Bridegroom's coming. However much we may want to, I cannot give you my preparation and you cannot give me yours. I can exhort you to prepare, I can encourage you as you prepare, as you can me, but I can't do it for you. All that God is weaving into me in terms of preparation in this life cannot be taken out of me and given to you. He is going to weave into your life your own preparation, as you allow Him. God weaves things into our lives, by way of preparation, that we may not like, yet when we think of it as our preparation for eternity we can more willingly co-operate. It is in our preparation that the reality of our relationship with God is evidenced. Why do I say that? Because to those who were not prepared, the Bridegroom said, 'I don't know you.'

How then can I make myself ready? In the life of my friend from the first couple I see evidence of her preparation for marriage:

Her engagement ring

On the third finger of her left hand she wears a lovely diamond ring, given to her by her fiancé. She gladly displays it and can often be found looking at it herself. The Holy Spirit is our engagement ring – He is the Spirit of our heavenly Bridegroom. It is the Holy Spirit who shows us how to prepare. 'But the Counsellor, the Holy Spirit, whom the Father will send in my name, will teach you all things and will remind you of everything I have said to you' (John 14:26).

In the story of Esther we read: 'When the turn came for Esther … to go to the king, she asked for nothing other than what Hegai, the king's eunuch who was in charge of the harem, suggested. And Esther won the favour of everyone who saw her' (Esth. 2:15). God's wisdom as to how to prepare is available to us, just as the wisdom of Hegai was available to Esther. She submitted herself totally to his guidance. Will we submit totally to the Lord's?

Time together

Understandably my friend wants to spend as much time as possible with her fiancé: time doing practical things together, time talking, time meeting others and more intimate times when the focus is on getting to know each other more deeply. It would be very strange if her attitude were: 'Well, I'm going to have to spend so much time with him when we are married that I'd prefer to do other things with my time now.' Sadly, this seems to be the attitude of some Christians towards spending time with their heavenly fiancé! It's as if they are planning an arranged marriage: the contract has been drawn up and signed, yet the relationship can wait until they meet at the altar. Might Jesus say, 'I never knew you'? This life is a wonderful opportunity to deepen our relationship with Jesus through talking with Him, working with Him, fellowshipping with others who know Him and worshipping Him. Why would anyone want to go to heaven and be married to Jesus without getting to know Him first?

The bottom drawer

It used to be the tradition for a young woman to have a 'bottom drawer': a place where she kept articles of clothing and household linen in preparation for marriage; items that she would take with her to her marital home. Even if we no longer have our 'bottom drawer' we still focus on 'the dress'. In Revelation 19:8 says 'Fine linen, bright and clean, was given her (the bride) to wear.' John goes on to explain: 'Fine linen stands for the righteous acts of the saints.' As one preacher put it, if the Church, the bride of Christ, is to wear a dress made from the righteous acts of the saints, there will only be enough material for a bikini! Isaiah is very clear what these righteous acts comprise:

Is not this the kind of fasting I have chosen: to loose the chains of injustice and untie the cords of the yoke, to set the oppressed free and break every yoke? Is it not to share your food with the hungry and to provide the poor wanderer with shelter – when you see the naked, to clothe him, and not to turn away from your own flesh and blood? Then your light will break forth like the dawn, and your healing quickly appear; then your righteousness will go before you, and the glory of the LORD will be your rear guard.

(Isa. 58:6–8)

These words are addressed to the people of God collectively. In our individualistic society we can be daunted, thinking, 'What can one person do?' Yet for the Church of God, equipped and empowered by the Spirit of God, nothing is impossible.

Changed language
My friend's language is changing from 'I' to 'we'. She increasingly thinks as a couple. This change of language represents a more fundamental change – the gradual death of her 'single' status with its entitlements to think, decide and act for herself, and the embracing of a 'united' status where her responsibility to her fiancé is reflected in joint decision-making and action. One Christian speaker says, 'I've learned to always say "we", referring to Jesus and me, except when confessing sin!' Jesus is clear that we show our love through obedience to His commands. This does not mean that we become robots whereby Jesus presses some mechanical switch and we turn right, turn left, stop etc. No, it's that we no longer want to make decisions on our own – we want and need His wisdom for every aspect of our lives.

Changed relationships
Most weekends, my friend and her fiancé spend their time visiting different friends and family members – they are keen that their relationships now include the other person. Sadly,

there are some friends whom I saw for the last time on their wedding day – I never had the opportunity to get to know their husbands before their marriage, and our friendship has not survived their changed circumstances. I long for my friends and family here on earth to share in the marriage of the Lamb and life in heaven. For that to happen, it is important that I introduce them to my prospective Bridegroom now! Some will not want to know Him, I realise that, but a shared eternity is worth the risk of some discomfort in our friendship now.

Energy for today

There is a lot to do in preparing for a wedding: a church and reception to be booked, a guest list drawn up, the invitations sent out, the dresses for bride and bridesmaids chosen and purchased, the flowers and photographer arranged, and so it goes on. All this is happening whilst 'normal' life continues for the engaged couple – work, shopping, eating, housework etc. Where does the extra energy come from? It seems to me that, tiring as all these preparations may seem to others, they carry with them an excitement that fills my friend with joy. She knows that they are all pointing to a future hope – the day when she will be a bride. It has been said that faith is hearing the music of the future and dancing to it today.

'Naming the day' appears to have given a focus, an energy and a direction to one friend's period of engagement that the other friend does not have. Similarly, I believe a right focus on heaven can transform how we live now. 'Let us hold unswervingly to the hope we profess, for he who promised is faithful. And let us consider how we may spur one another on towards love and good deeds. Let us not give up meeting together, as some are in the habit of doing, but let us encourage one another – and all the more as you see the Day approaching' (Heb. 10:23–25).

The bride

We waited expectantly for the bride to arrive – my good friend was getting married. Watching her process down the aisle I was surprised – my friend would not normally turn heads, but on her wedding day she was radiant! It wasn't just the beautiful dress, it was her. Growing in relationship with her fiancé, she had prepared herself for this day; and now the full force of her love, joy and preparation radiated from her being. Her future husband awaited her at the altar, his tear-filled eyes glowing as he beheld his bride. He too had longed for this day and his delight in his wife was evident.

In Ephesians we are told that human marriage is a reflection of the marriage of Christ to His Church. How will we look on that day? Glorious! 'And we, who with unveiled faces all reflect the Lord's glory, are being transformed into his likeness with ever-increasing glory …' (2 Cor. 3:18). At the bridal supper of the Lamb the transformation will be complete – we will again reflect the image of God. The image that Eve reflected at creation, marred by the Fall, redeemed by Christ's death, will be restored – His bride is ready.

A wedding isn't the end of the story, it's the start of a marriage where 'the dwelling of God is with men … They will be his people, and God himself will be with them …' (Rev. 21:3).

You are a woman – an image-bearer of the living God. Right now you may feel that the treasure of God's image is well hidden in an earthen vessel, but one day it will be revealed. Jesus has chosen you from the creation of the world to be His – He has pursued you, redeemed you, wooed you and one day will wed you. You are precious and honoured in His sight. He alone knows your true beauty and has given you His life in order that you might fulfil your role as a godly woman who laughs at the days to come, brings good not harm, is a life-bearer and sustainer, whose hand is trained for battle and who marches to a different drum. Your heavenly Bridegroom requires your presence beside Him in this world and the one to come. Will you take your God-given place?

For reflection

- What things cause you to think about heaven?

- In what ways does the knowledge of heaven impact you day to day?

- How has the Holy Spirit led you to prepare?

Notes

Introduction

1. Matthew Henry, *Commentary on the Whole Bible* (Edinburgh: Alban Books/Hendrickson Publishers, 1994).
2. First published in *Pocket Prayers for Work* compiled by Mark Greene, LICC (London: Church House Publishing, 2004). Copyright © Beverley Shepherd

Chapter 1

1. *Captivating*, John & Stasi Eldredge (Nashville: Nelson Books, 2005) pp.134–135.
2. *When nothing you ever do seems to satisfy*, Selwyn Hughes (Eastbourne: Kingsway Publications, 1994) p.29.
3. *The Everlasting God*, D. Broughton Knox (Darlington: Evangelical Press, 1982)
4. *Men & Women*, Lawrence J. Crabb (London: Marshal Pickering, 1991) p.198.
5. *The Illustrated Bible Dictionary* (Leicester: IVP, 1980)
6. *Men & Women*, Lawrence J. Crabb (London: Marshall Pickering, 1991) p.207.
7. I am indebted to John & Stasi Eldredge in *Captivating* (op. cit.) for this information.

Chapter 2

1. *When nothing you ever do seems to satisfy*, Selwyn Hughes (Eastbourne: Kingsway, 1994) p.72.
2. Ibid, p.32.
3. Adapted from *A Dose of Salt*, Simon Coupland (Crowborough: Monarch Publications, 1997)
4. *City of Gold*, Adrian Plass (Carlisle: Paternoster Publishing, 1997)

Chapter 3

1. *Matthew*, Charles Price (Fearn, Ross-shire: Christian Focus Publications, 1998)

2. *Contributions to Christian Feminism*, Elaine Storkey (London: Christian Impact Ltd., 1995) p.18.
3. *Alive in Christ*, Charles Price (Grand Rapids: Kregel Publications, 1995) p.83.
4. Adapted from *The Naked Life*, Duncan Banks (Grand Rapids: Zondervan, 2004).

Chapter 4

1. *The Call*, Os Guinness (Nashville: Word Publishing, 1998).
2. *The Life of the Beloved*, Henri J.M. Nouwen (London: Hodder & Stoughton, 1993) pp.44–45.
3. Ibid pp.37,39.
4. *The True Vine*, Andrew Murray (Aylesbury: Rickfords Hill Publishing Ltd, 2003) p.22.
5. 'When we walk with the Lord', John Henry Sammis, Methodist Hymn Book (Aylesbury: Hazell Watson & Viney Ltd, 1933).
6. *The Divine Conspiracy*, Dallas Willard (London: Fount Paperbacks, 1998) p.58.
7. Ibid. p.58.
8. *The Life of the Beloved*, Henri J.M. Nouwen (London: Hodder & Stoughton, 1993) p.62.
9. *The True Vine*, Andrew Murray (Aylesbury: Rickfords Hill Publishing Ltd., 2003) p.34.
10. *Hudson Taylor's Spiritual Secret*, Dr. & Mrs. Howard Taylor (Grand Rapids: Discovery House Publishers, 1990).

Chapter 5

1. *Provocations: Spiritual Writings of Søren Kierkegaard* edited by Charles E. Moore (Maryknoll, N.Y.: Orbis, 2003).
2. *Christ for Real*, Charles W. Price (Grand Rapids: Kregel Publications, 1995).
3. *The Secret Message of Jesus*, Brian McLaren (Nashville: W Publishing Group, 2006) pp.132–133.
4. *Waking the Dead*, John Eldredge (Nashville: Thomas Nelson Inc. 2003) pp.18,38.
5. *Contributions to Christian Feminism*, Elaine Storkey (London, Christian Impact Ltd., 1995) pp.87–88.
6. *The Secret Message of Jesus*, Brian McLaren (Nashville: W Publishing Group, 2006) p.134.

Chapter 6

1. *Spoken from the Heart*, Selwyn Hughes (Farnham: CWR, 2005) p.136.
2. *Jesus Rediscovered*, Malcolm Muggeridge (Collins: Fontana, 1969)
3. *Heaven Bound*, Selwyn Hughes (Farnham: CWR, 2003) p.35.
4. *My Story*, Selwyn Hughes (Farnham: CWR, 2004) p.383.

National Distributors

UK: (and countries not listed below)
CWR, Waverley Abbey House, Waverley Lane, Farnham, Surrey GU9 8EP.
Tel: (01252) 784700 Outside UK (44) 1252 784700

AUSTRALIA: CMC Australasia, PO Box 519, Belmont, Victoria 3216.
Tel: (03) 5241 3288 Fax: (03) 5241 3290

CANADA: Cook Communications Ministries, PO Box 98, 55 Woodslee Avenue, Paris, Ontario N3L 3E5.
Tel: 1800 263 2664

GHANA: Challenge Enterprises of Ghana, PO Box 5723, Accra.
Tel: (021) 222437/223249 Fax: (021) 226227

HONG KONG: Cross Communications Ltd, 1/F, 562A Nathan Road, Kowloon.
Tel: 2780 1188 Fax: 2770 6229

INDIA: Crystal Communications, 10-3-18/4/1, East Marredpalli, Secunderabad – 500026, Andhra Pradesh.
Tel/Fax: (040) 27737145

KENYA: Keswick Books and Gifts Ltd, PO Box 10242, Nairobi. Tel: (02) 331692/226047
Fax: (02) 728557

MALAYSIA: Salvation Book Centre (M) Sdn Bhd, 23 Jalan SS 2/64, 47300 Petaling Jaya, Selangor.
Tel: (03) 78766411/78766797 Fax: (03) 78757066/78756360

NEW ZEALAND: CMC Australasia, PO Box 303298, North Harbour, Auckland 0751.
Tel: 0800 449 408 Fax: 0800 449 049

NIGERIA: FBFM, Helen Baugh House, 96 St Finbarr's College Road, Akoka, Lagos.
Tel: (01) 7747429/4700218/825775/827264

PHILIPPINES: OMF Literature Inc, 776 Boni Avenue, Mandaluyong City.
Tel: (02) 531 2183 Fax: (02) 531 1960

SINGAPORE: Alby Commercial Enterprises Pte Ltd, 95 Kallang Avenue #04-00, AIS Industrial Building, 339420.
Tel: (65) 629 27238 Fax: (65) 629 27235

SOUTH AFRICA: Struik Christian Books, 80 MacKenzie Street, PO Box 1144, Cape Town 8000.
Tel: (021) 462 4360 Fax: (021) 461 3612

SRI LANKA: Christombu Publications (Pvt) Ltd, Bartleet House, 65 Braybrooke Place, Colombo 2.
Tel: (9411) 2421073/2447665

TANZANIA: CLC Christian Book Centre, PO Box 1384, Mkwepu Street, Dar es Salaam.
Tel/Fax: (022) 2119439

USA: Cook Communications Ministries, PO Box 98, 55 Woodslee Avenue, Paris, Ontario N3L 3E5, Canada.
Tel: 1800 263 2664

ZIMBABWE: Word of Life Books (Pvt) Ltd, Christian Media Centre, 8 Aberdeen Road, Avondale, PO Box A480
Avondale, Harare. Tel: (04) 333355 or 091301188

For email addresses, visit the CWR website: www.cwr.org.uk

CWR is a Registered Charity – Number 294387

CWR is a Limited Company registered in England – Registration Number 1990308

Day and Residential Courses
Counselling Training
Leadership Development
Biblical Study Courses
Regional Seminars
Ministry to Women
Daily Devotionals
Books and Videos
Conference Centre

Trusted all Over the World

CWR HAS GAINED A WORLDWIDE reputation as a centre of excellence for Bible-based training and resources. From our headquarters at Waverley Abbey House, Farnham, England, we have been serving God's people for over 40 years with a vision to help apply God's Word to everyday life and relationships. The daily devotional *Every Day with Jesus* is read by nearly a million readers an issue in more than 150 countries, and our unique courses in biblical studies and pastoral care are respected all over the world. Waverley Abbey House provides a conference centre in a tranquil setting.

For free brochures on our seminars and courses, conference facilities, or a catalogue of CWR resources, please contact us at the following address:
CWR, Waverley Abbey House, Waverley Lane, Farnham, Surrey GU9 8EP, UK

Telephone: +44 (0)1252 784700
Email: mail@cwr.org.uk
Website: www.cwr.org.uk

 Applying God's Word
to everyday life and relationships

Inspiring Women: Finding Freedom

In this challenging and exciting book Helena Wilkinson shows us how it is only in surrendering ourselves, our time, finances, possessions, work and activity to God that we encounter the deepest joy and freedom. The closer we walk with Him the more we will become like Him and reflect His character.

£6.99
ISBN: 978-1-85345-451-6

Inspiring Women Every Day

This life-enriching daily devotional written by women for women is a source of inspiration and encouragement to all ages. It will help you find practical support to face the challenges of living; encourage you through the insightful guidance of Scripture; and build your faith with daily readings from the Bible.

£2.25 each
£12.50 UK annual subscription
ISSN: 1478-050X

Inspiring Women Every Day Compact Bible

A Holman Christian Standard Bible in a portable format, with a bonded-leather cover, gilt-edged with two ribbon markers and the words of Jesus in red, presented in a protective slipcase. It includes an additional 30-day devotional section focusing on 'Daughters of the King' written by an *Inspiring Women Every Day* author.

£17.99
ISBN: 978-1-85345-401-1